FIVE PILLARS OF THE FREEDOM LIFESTYLE

HOW TO ESCAPE YOUR
COMFORT ZONE OF MISERY

FIVE PILLARS OF THE

Freedom

LIFESTYLE

Superpowers • Vision • Alignment • Outcomes • Flow

CURT MERCADANTE

LIONCREST
PUBLISHING

FIVE PILLARS OF THE FREEDOM LIFESTYLE

How to Escape Your Comfort Zone of Misery

ISBN   978-1-5445-0384-4 *Hardcover*

978-1-5445-0382-0 *Paperback*

978-1-5445-0383-7 *Ebook*

For my wife, Julie, who inspires and empowers me.

To my children, Anna, Dominic, Rocco, and
Santino, who teach me every day.

To my parents, who taught me not to take shit from anybody.

CONTENTS

Part I

INTRO

As I lay there in bed, staring at the ceiling, it felt just like any other workday. The problem was, it wasn't a workday. It was the Tuesday of Thanksgiving week, and it was supposed to be my day off.

Had I informed all my clients? Of course. But that didn't stop them from calling, requesting memos and emails, asking me to hop on conference calls. There also was the issue about the client-planning meeting I was supposed to attend the following week.

In that same meeting the year before, we had been scolded like children for being "low energy." It was an 8:30 a.m. meeting on a Monday, in frigid Washington, DC, temperatures, for which I had to fly in the night before...a Sunday. While I sat there being scolded with the rest of my client team, I vowed never again to attend this meeting.

Time passed, however, and I settled back in to my comfort zone—afraid to rock the boat and threaten my healthy retainer. But something broke in me this Tuesday morning of Thanksgiving week.

I decided then and there to shut down my seven-figure PR/ad agency at peak revenue.

As I approached my wife, Julie, to break the news, the

butterflies danced in my stomach. The sweat coated my now clammy palms. What was she going to say? Would she be upset? After all, we have four kids, a mortgage, two cars, and a life.

I decided to make it quick. Short, simple, and sweet.

"Jules, I can't take it anymore," I blurted out. "I'm done."

Julie gazed into my eyes. No anger in hers. No panic. She reached out and touched my arm. "It's about time," she replied. And we hugged.

That was it. Thirteen years of building a successful agency, and now it was over.

Had I made a bunch of money? Absolutely. Had I built two profitable businesses? Yep. But it wasn't worth the corresponding pain. I had built a prison instead of a business.

Now, it was time to turn my coaching side hustle into my full-time gig. Sink or swim. No life preserver.

Scary? Yes. But it was also exhilarating—the thought of helping others avoid the mistakes I had made while building my business.

Fast-forward to today. I've coached hundreds of people.

Clients around the world. Millions of views of videos I've created (mostly on LinkedIn) meant to teach and provide value. All of it done with the vision of helping individuals fight for lives of freedom and fulfillment.

That's the reason I wrote this book.

We business owners start our businesses, sometimes leaving "stable" nine-to-five careers to do so, because we want our freedom. Nobody watching over our shoulders. Nobody requiring us to be sitting at our desks by 8:30 a.m. No long commutes. No bosses.

However, too many business owners, like me, build prisons instead of businesses. The freedom they desire seems out of reach. The extra time they thought they'd have with their family and friends never materializes. What do they get instead? Less vacation time. Longer hours. Clients who disrespect them.

Entrepreneurial freedom doesn't just mean starting your own business. True entrepreneurial freedom means growing your business while growing your freedom and fulfillment. It means aligning your work with your family and you.

During the past year, date nights with my wife, special days with my kids, our two-week journey through California, and our five-week tour across Europe stand out to me more than any work accomplishment I achieved this past year. I'd like you to feel the same way about your year.

Through my experience building three profitable companies and coaching and speaking to hundreds of entrepreneurs, I've come up with the Freedom Five—five key areas that must be firing on all cylinders to give you true entrepreneurial freedom:

1. **Superpowers:** Are you amplifying your true strengths and managing your weaknesses?
2. **Vision:** Do you have a clear vision that combines your purpose and impact?
3. **Alignment:** Are you aligning your work with your family and self?
4. **Outcomes:** Are you reverse engineering your vision to create detailed, simple yearly/monthly/weekly/daily outcomes?
5. **Flow:** Are you bringing these all together so that you're flowing, not grinding, every single day?

Yes, these are the five pillars of the Freedom Lifestyle mentioned in the title of this book, and we get into each of them in great detail. First, however, it's necessary to recognize some of the warning signs that show you might be lacking the freedom you desire.

"If I lack freedom, wouldn't I know it?" you ask. Not necessarily.

It's easy to confuse numbers in a bank account for freedom, to remember that last good vacation you had with your family (even though it was two years ago) and mistake it for fulfillment, or to rationalize the long nights and anxiety in the name of a paycheck.

That's denial. And it's unhealthy.

This book is separated into two sections. Part 1 deals with the warning signs and symptoms you may be feeling of a life without true freedom. Part 2 delves into the Freedom Five. At the end of this book, there's a call to action for you to find your Freedom Index to learn the level of freedom in your life—with the opportunity to take action today to start living the Freedom Lifestyle you desire.

It's a journey you deserve. It's an outcome you desire. Let's take it together.

CHAPTER 1

A COMFORT ZONE OF MISERY

My left arm went numb, and I had tingling in my fingertips. Shortness of breath. Then the stomach pains began. Pain so bad I was curled in the fetal position on my bed.

The lights were off, and I was in my bed. My wife cracked open the door to check on me, and I asked her if she could please move the kids to the basement. We only had two kids at the time, and they weren't being bad; they were just playing.

The noise, however, was too much for me to bear.

I felt ashamed and guilty to admit it, but I was having an anxiety attack.

What did I have to feel guilty about? A seven-figure agency; two wonderful kids; a beautiful, loving wife; a great house. I'm a man, and I was doing what I was supposed to do. Anxiety attack? Forget it. I'm supposed to tough this shit out.

So I did.

To be sure, I made some changes. More delegation at work so I could become more productive and work fewer hours. A new diet and healthy lifestyle that focused on a "primal" lifestyle with lower carbs, natural animal protein, and plant-based foods—no grains or dairy and less sugar. I replaced chronic, long-distance cardio with higher-intensity sprint workouts.

All of that helped.

My weight dropped from 205 to the 160s. I had been on a statin cholesterol drug for eight years, and I was able to ditch it. The stomach pains subsided.

In short, I gained more freedom in my life. More time to spend with my family. Less time worrying about my physical appearance, and more importantly, less physical pain. But something was still missing. I had gained some freedom, but I still lacked fulfillment in my life.

The guilt increased.

I had always been taught that a healthy dose of gratitude is essential to a happy life. So I focused on the fact that I should be happy because I have it better than so many people in the world. A roof over my head. Two cars. Not living paycheck to paycheck.

This was all accurate. I should've been grateful for all that I had. But I was using gratitude as an excuse for not wanting more.

QUIET DESPERATION

Henry David Thoreau wrote, "The mass of men lead lives of quiet desperation."

When I was in high school, I rejected Thoreau's writings. Especially *Walden*. I wanted glitz. Glamour. Income. Money. Why the hell would anyone want to move to a quiet lake? The older I get, however, the more I identify with him.

Upon first reading, one might think "quiet desperation" describes someone who is outwardly unhappy, depressed, or just plain funky. Not so.

In fact, he was describing how I felt for years. Now, I describe that "quiet desperation" as living in a "comfort zone of misery." Outwardly, everything seems fine. In reality, it's "blah." No passion. No excitement. And yes, despite what Thoreau wrote, many women live the same way.

Clinging on to stability instead of reaching for greatness. Putting off dreams and desires to aggressively protect the status quo.

Tony Robbins wrote, "Change happens when the pain of staying the same is greater than the pain of change." That's why this comfort zone, this quiet-desperation status, is so dangerous. The pain isn't acute but, rather, more like a dull ache. We can put up with it for years—and we often do.

Our fear of rocking the boat of our lifestyle, our paycheck, or our external expectations keeps us trapped, sometimes for years. I get it. I really do. I was once there. Trapped in that comfort zone. The lock on my prison-cell door was forged from the gold of a successful agency and killer revenue.

But the quiet desperation became very loud. Screaming at me. And so I escaped. Now, my mission is to help others do the same.

When I finally shut down my agency, I was scared as hell. But it's funny—I haven't had an anxiety attack since. No more waking up with dread. I have a business with clients I love and a mission that fulfills me. I have work that is aligned with my family and me. There are days that are challenges, days that suck. But now I'm in the driver's seat, with a clear vision and a life of freedom and fulfillment.

The point of this book is to help you do the same.

GRATITUDE

"I felt like suicide was the only answer. I had one last ounce (of hope), and that saved me."

—TOFE EVANS

In his midtwenties, making good money as an engineer, partying with his friends, doing hard and soft drugs alike—that's what Tofe Evans's life had become.

It was a life of pleasure without meaning. As can happen, the pleasure masked the true pain, leading to a life of quiet desperation. That desperation, however, continued to build, until it became deafening and caused Tofe to feel like he had lost all hope.

In Tofe's mind, the solution was clear: ending his life.

"I didn't know what I was doing with my life," Tofe told me. "I was also an engineer for eight years, funnily enough. I didn't know what I was doing, and I ended up struggling really bad with depression and anxiety for almost a year. It honestly felt like suicide was the only answer."

Tofe isn't alone. Anxiety, depression, and suicidal thoughts affect millions of people around the world— people of all races, nations, economic levels, and faith traditions.

How do you move from a state of depression so deep that suicide is a viable option to living your life with purpose and enthusiasm?

One word: gratitude.

"At the end of the day, it's even being grateful for the little things," Tofe said, "and it's being grateful amidst the chaos, being grateful for that moment. For example, I'm driving, and my car hasn't had air conditioning in two years. It's very hot in the Gold Coast [Australia, where he lives] in summer. I'm getting to meetings sweaty, so I just wear black shirts. In that midst, it's just going, Tofe, just be grateful you have a car."

To be fair, there are many who adopt an attitude of gratitude. It's an attitude that is drilled into us since we are young.

"Be grateful for what you have."

"Eat everything on your plate because there are starving children in [insert country name] who would be happy to have your food."

It's easy, however, to use gratitude as an excuse not to push for greatness. On a weekly basis, I run into people who do just that.

They call me because they are lacking fulfillment in their lives and they want help, but they feel guilty. They have a good paycheck, a nice car, and a roof over their heads.

They tell me their life "isn't that bad," that others have it worse than they do.

Let's be clear: there are always going to be people who have it worse than you. If you have people who love you, a home—if you're alive—you should be grateful. But don't you dare hide behind that as an excuse not to fight for more in your life.

Tofe Evans sure didn't. He paired gratitude with massive action. It propelled him forward, and he accomplished some pretty extraordinary achievements, including more than one hundred ultramarathons, including one across

Mt. Everest. He also recently published his book, *Everyone Has a Plan Until Sh!t Hits the Fan.*

"You've got to do something," he said. "Just defy the odds."

Do something. Do anything. It's the only place to start. But as many of us know, starting isn't finishing. We don't move from deep depression to doing ultramarathons and writing books in weeks. What happens between starting and finishing?

For Tofe, it was doing something he'd never done before: marathons.

"I started focusing on running," said Tofe. "I told my friend, 'I think I'm going to run a marathon.'"

He and his friend had been drinking, so his friend thought it was a joke. But for Tofe, it was a pledge to improve his life through disciplined training.

"I looked up how much time it takes to train for a marathon. It says sixteen weeks. I had seventeen weeks. I said, 'This may be a good sign.' I paid for it and thought, I have to do it now. I paid for it."

"I did the training and you know what? When you do four months of training, you are going to make new habits.

I thought, This is amazing. I'm literally the fittest and healthiest I've been in a long time."

Several years and thousands of miles later, he's still focused on gratitude.

He told me of a situation in which he was running a race at twenty thousand feet. It was two in the morning, and he had been going for twenty hours straight.

"My headlight is starting to run out of batteries. I can't see, and I have to really engage and focus because if I trip, I'm going to eat shit so hard," he recalled. "It got to a point where I needed to sleep, so I found a local bush and took a four-minute nap. It's like I tricked my brain into believing I had a decent sleep. At the end of the race, I was just grateful that I had some food."

Gratitude and action.

INFRASTRUCTURE-RATTLING EVENTS

Tofe paired gratitude with action to dig himself out of his hole and save his life. But why did it take him getting so close to the bottom before he made a change?

In an interview on my podcast, entrepreneur and podcaster Tim Alison introduced me to the term "infrastructure-rattling event." He explained that the term was used by consultant/coach Kevin Bulmer on Tim's podcast to explain those situations that sometimes are required to force change in our lives.

"I'm approaching my midforties, and anybody who's in that age group with whom I've spoken reports something very similar in terms of going down the path of life the way that they really perceived that they were supposed to be doing it," Bulmer told Alison on the latter's *Screw the Naysayers* podcast. "Ending up bewildered, lost, frustrated, or in my case, it was a divorce, ill health, business failing—some sort of *infrastructure-rattling* foundational change that you either change, or, what I might suggest the majority of people do, which is to keep, just keep jumping back into the same bear trap" (italics added).

Having experienced such a "rattling" event, Bulmer did make a change and is now an international public speaker, mindset coach, and host of the *Journeys of the No Schedule Man* podcast.

Tofe Evans faced his "rattling" event in the form of being close to suicide, but he made his change as well. Sometimes it just takes such a foundational earthquake to wake us up and force us to change the trajectory of our lives.

The anxiety and feelings of overwhelm and frustration I

felt midway through my journey of building my PR and ad agency should have been such an event for me, but they weren't. Well, not quite.

To be sure, I made some positive changes, using Gallup's CliftonStrengths program to help me work within my strengths at work and become more productive. This helped me gain some freedom in my work life.

There still, however, were problems. The anxiety attacks were fewer and farther between, but they were still there. I continued to have that feeling that I wasn't doing what I was put on this earth to do. The feelings of guilt continued, and I used gratitude as an excuse to remain trapped in my comfort zone of misery.

That's when my infrastructure-rattling event happened. My father passed away in 2012 after a two-year fight against prostate and bladder cancer.

My dad had been my hero. My counselor. The rock that held our family together. Even when I lived a thousand miles away, I still felt his presence guiding me through my work and nonwork life. When he passed away, I began a downward mental spiral.

My dad had an incredible career. He worked on the space program, and after he passed, we dug up a thank-you letter from Honeywell corporation thanking him for his work on the Mars Mariner 6 and 7 spacecraft that took photos of the equator and southern hemisphere of Mars. He helped design electronics on fighter jets and led the team that designed all the electronic switches on the Boeing 777 aircraft.

In my eyes, he was a real-life superhero, a real-life Tony Stark—the secret identity of Marvel superhero Iron Man.

Sitting at his wake, however, something became very clear. I watched as men in their seventies recalled stories about my dad with tears streaming down their faces. Everyone had some story about my dad and the impact he had on them, their organizations, or their communities.

Yet, nary a person talked about anything from my dad's career.

The stories were all about him as a father and husband, his volunteer work dictating audiobooks for the blind or working with a local housing charity, his role in the University of Notre Dame Alumni Association, or his work at our church.

It was like a glass of cold water thrown in my face. What was I doing? My dad had clearly set the example for me, and I was ignoring it—so focused only on work and career that the other parts of my life were suffering.

It dawned on me that I had created some freedom with my business, but I fundamentally lacked fulfillment in my life. So I decided to make a change. I had no idea what that change meant, but I knew it had to happen.

Around that time, friends and colleagues had asked me to begin coaching them. After all, I had built a profitable business, they wanted some help, and I obliged. It quickly became apparent to me that not only was I a good coach, but I was far more fulfilled from coaching than I was from my work for my agency clients.

I would not want s.o. who is unhappy w/ his own business to be my coach.

The agency, however, was still paying the bills, so I never seriously considered dropping it to coach full time. In my head, I had the goal of "someday" ramping down my agency and ramping up my coaching. It was a vague goal with no set milestones—until the day I described in the introduction of this book—the day I decided to shutter my agency and coach full time.

Eric Malzone, who is now a digital nomad, mentor, podcast host, and founder of the Fitness Accelerator, recently told me of the infrastructure-rattling events in his life that spurred him and his wife to make a change and live the Freedom Lifestyle.

"Everyone in their life is going to have that *thing*, right?" Malzone asked me. "That thing that happens where it changes who you are, where it was so challenging you didn't think you were going to come out of it. And if you don't know what that *thing* is yet, it hasn't happened, because you don't get through this life unscathed.

"For us, it was, you know, in 2016 we got pregnant, but as things progressed, things weren't looking good. Ultimately, we lost the pregnancy late, at twenty weeks. And that was extremely traumatizing, especially for my wife. It was rough. And then after that, about two months later, her father passed away of a heart attack at sixty-one. Then we had another friend who passed away at the age of forty. And then, at the end of it, our dog died."

After all of that loss in a single year, "My chemistry just shifted," said Malzone. "The things I enjoyed weren't the same anymore. Things that used to not stress me out, stressed me out."

When I introduced the term "infrastructure-rattling event" to Eric, he said that's exactly how he felt.

"Whatever that event is, it never goes away," he said, adding that you can find power in these situations, maybe helping other people going through similar situations, or you adapt your mindset so that what you thought was rough before doesn't even compare to what you've already been through.

"Gratitude comes from it too," Malzone added.

Malzone said he and his wife were awakened by this tragic year. He sold his successful and profitable Cross-Fit gym in Santa Barbara, launched his podcasts and an online accelerator for fitness professionals, the Fitness Accelerator, and he and his wife hit the road, becoming digital nomads. When I spoke with Eric, they were currently living in Whitefish, Montana, for a six-month spell. At the end of six months, they'd reevaluate and either stay or move on to another region.

Does everyone who faces such infrastructure-rattling events use it as a similar life awakening, as happened to Tofe, Eric, or me? Of course not.

"There are all sorts of people who are miserable, but they've become very good actors at convincing both themselves and others that it's not true," said Tim Alison. "If that doesn't work anymore, they go into victim mode, where it's not their fault, and there's also nothing they can do about it."

Alison is absolutely correct, and he's explaining that comfort zone of misery and quiet desperation I explained at the beginning of this chapter. The point of this book, however, isn't to examine why some people retreat to that zone but, rather, how you can spur yourself on to a life awakening before your infrastructure gets rattled.

LIVING A LIE

Caleb Campbell was born in a hospital where a small football was put in the crib of every newborn boy.

"The Texas Panhandle," he told me in an interview on my podcast. "I grew up in a small Texas town, nine thousand people. The closest Walmart was forty-five minutes away, and the closest shopping mall and airport was two hours away."

This is football country. Serious football country.

"Football, at one point in my life, it was a game that I loved, and it was a game that I enjoyed playing," said Campbell. "It was a game that I, I think, naturally thrived in. I had a natural instinct, and I had a lot of speed, and it just was a good fit for me."

Caleb, however, was a "dedicated Christian boy" and though he was one of the best athletes in school, he said he was also one of the most bullied. This took a toll.

"I was incredibly suicidal in my high school years. Yeah, I was incredibly suicidal," he said. "I always was tormented with thoughts of *Is this worth it? Come on, what is going on?*"

During his sophomore and junior years in high school,

football transitioned from something he loved to something that allowed him to escape the torment and pain.

"I learned that if I'm scoring touchdowns on the football field, I leave that night, and people love me," he said. "I go out there and I run fast, I hit people, I score touchdowns. I make people scream and yell, and we win football games."

Football was no longer a game that he was able to enjoy. It was no longer an opportunity to excel. It was no longer a time where Caleb got to build friendships and community around a game. It wasn't that anymore. At this time, it became a means of escape.

Caleb propelled his team to the state championship, and he was inducted into the Texas High School Hall of Fame.

"Suddenly now, this is where people are accepting me," he said. "They're applauding me. They're loving me. It [football] is literally my lifeline. That became bondage in and of itself."

Caleb had a breakout sophomore year and began receiving offers to play at Division 1 schools. The Panhandle doesn't get as much recruiting interest as other parts of Texas, so many bigger schools stayed away. But not the United States Military Academy, also known as West Point.

"I took a visit, and I'm sitting there thinking, Oh my gosh, this is amazing," said Campbell. "That's when I realized that West Point was what I wanted to do."

He went on to have a stellar career at West Point, gaining a starting position his freshman year, and despite a knee injury his junior year, becoming the fourth- or fifth-rated strong safety in all of college football.

"My sophomore year is when a lot of professional scouts started coming around, and a lot of agents started calling me," he said. "A lot of people wanted to know what my deal was because of my involvement with West Point."

At the same time, he said he was a "very, very wounded person" who was "very hurt, very guarded, and very self-protected." After his experience in high school, he was desperate to have friends, and football continued to provide his means to get there.

"I was just so driven by fear and so driven by pain that it's not cool to say, but people at West Point, cadets at West Point, knew not to talk to me unless I talked to you. I was a big name on campus because of football, but I was just like, 'Don't talk to me,'" he said. "I wasn't a nice person."

Campbell ended up getting drafted in the seventh round of the NFL draft by the Detroit Lions.

"I get drafted. I drive home that day, and I get to West Point. My friends are there to celebrate with me and everything. We're eating pizza. You can't drink on campus, so we're just hanging out," said Campbell.

"I remember going to my room, Curt, and going to shower and curling up in a fetal position and just sobbing," he explained. "The pressure hit me that so many people are watching me."

"What if I don't make it? How am I going to find love in this life and value in this life? I'm going to be all alone."

Those were the thoughts that filled his head. He said he was living with this tension and constant self-dialogue and not sharing any of it with any friends or family.

On the day of his contract signing, and the day before training camp was supposed to begin, he got a phone call from the US Department of Defense. A previous department policy that would've allowed pro athletes like him to defer military service had been rescinded, and he was ordered into active duty immediately.

"I was apologetic to Detroit. The Detroit Lions missed out on a draft pick. They lost a draft pick," he said. "But I went back to my hotel room and just breathed a sigh of relief."

He put on a different act for the television networks, speaking of duty and pride. But internally, he was feeling something much different.

"In reality, I'm like, Ah, yes!" he said. "I don't have to run the risk of being the failure, of being exposed as this kid who doesn't have what it takes, and I get the whole world loving on me because they think I just got robbed."

After fulfilling his military service, Campbell returned to the NFL and the Detroit Lions, where he served on the practice squad. He also spent similar stints with the Indianapolis Colts and the Kansas City Chiefs.

Campbell told me he would purposely not give his all in practice, preferring to remain on the practice squad so he could reap the benefits of being an NFL player while never actually having to play in games.

In the end, it became too much for him, and he turned down additional offers and steady money to leave the NFL and commit a year of his life to a church in Fort Erie, Ontario. He spent that time dealing with, as he puts it, "with the fear of rejection" that haunted him, the "fear of never measuring up" that robbed him of his happiness, and the "fear of living an insignificant life."

Today, he spends his time serving at the church, speaking around the country, and helping run a marketing and design agency in Buffalo, New York.

"I fight fear and doubt daily," he said. "But I've never been happier."

After years of convincing himself that football was his life, fueled by the fear of failure and insignificance, Caleb is now helping others to overcome the challenges in their lives.

Like many of us, he spent years living a lie. Years in denial.

How can we avoid these years of pain?

What are the warning signs that we are living a life without freedom and fulfillment?

Let's explore that now.

CHAPTER 2

YOUR FREEDOM INDEX

"My son was two at the time, and he looked me in the eye and said, 'Dad, why are you always grumpy?'"

—FRASER CAMERON

At the time of the writing of this book, Fraser Cameron, his wife, and two young children are in the midst of a yearlong adventure of traveling throughout France. Originally from Auckland, New Zealand, the French adventure was a longtime dream of the Cameron clan.

In his younger days, Fraser had been one of the top sprinters in New Zealand. But years of the corporate grind as a commercial negotiation consultant had added pounds to his frame, slowing his steps and placing him firmly in a comfort zone of misery. He never wavered in his love for his wife, Kelly, and their son and daughter, but he was going through the motions and didn't even realize it.

"My wife and my kids weren't getting the best version of me," he explained.

Until the day his son's comment changed his life.

"I had come home from a long day at the office, having battled traffic, having battled the other zombies who were frustrated at work," he said, explaining that's when his son asked him why he was always grumpy.

"Talk about a metaphorical slap to the face," said Fraser. "You don't often realize it until you get that retrospective chance to look back at how you were. But I was always grumpy. I was really unhappy. I was frustrated. I was stuck. I wasn't doing what I wanted, when I wanted, how I wanted.

"And unfortunately, I was taking it out on the people who mattered the most to me. My wife and my kids weren't getting the best version of me. And for a two-year-old to come out with a comment like that, that was so sobering."

His son's comment ripped back the curtain and allowed Fraser to have an honest look at what had become a grumpy grind of a life. It made him realize that he was completely stuck.

"I was the complete antithesis of free, and it really resonated with me, and it really prompted me into significant and drastic action."

So, what did he do?

"I went in to work the next day and quit. I literally packed up my things and said goodbye," he said.

Today, in addition to accompanying his family on their French adventure, Fraser is a coach and creator of the #EpicDads program, helping dads create opportunity and choice so they can enjoy more time, freedom, and fulfillment.

In 2017, inspired by his story, I not only hired Fraser as my personal coach, but my family—including my wife and four kids—traveled to Europe for a five-week vacation and met up with Fraser's family just outside Paris. He is now my lifelong friend.

Fraser and I connect from our similar experiences, but we also see and help people every week who also have been living for years in quiet desperation. We are both touched and saddened by those who know they need change but would rather wait for the pain to increase to force their hands.

We also know that there are millions of individuals out

there who are stuck in lives of quiet desperation and don't even know it. They think it's totally normal.

If you're reading this book, you probably have an inkling that you're lacking the freedom you desire. Even so, you may not be entirely clear what that means or what it will take to achieve the Freedom Lifestyle.

That's why I created the Freedom Index. Ten simple statements that, if you consider them honestly, will provide you with a clear view of what and where freedom is lacking in your life.

The Freedom Index statements are laid out below, and you are invited to rate them each on a scale of 1–10, with a 10 meaning you strongly agree with the statement. You can also visit my website—CurtMercadante.com— to complete the questionnaire, be provided your Index score, and determine if you want to take further action to transform your lifestyle.

1—MY DAYS ARE FILLED WITH THINGS I WANT TO DO VS. THINGS I FEEL COMPELLED TO DO

A potential client once told me that he and his wife were not fulfilled, that he didn't have time to do the things he loved, such as play music and write, and that they spent all their free time driving their kids from sporting event to sporting event. He apologized, however, saying, "I know this is just the normal course of life."

Nope. Sorry. Perhaps society has made you believe that a life of compulsion is the normal course of life, but it is not. If you honestly feel like you don't have a say—a choice—in how you spend your days, you are not living a life of freedom.

Each of us comes out of the womb with a sense of wonder, a desire for exploration and discovery, even if it's simply exploring the world on the back porch, behind the couch, or under the table. Somewhere along the way, however, that sense of wonder and discovery is squeezed out of us.

At a young age, our life becomes about getting into the best kindergarten (yes, parents are competing to get their five-year-old kids into schools), then the best elementary school, the best junior high, the college prep high school, and then, of course, to a specific college where we should adopt a specific major that will guarantee a job and happiness for the rest of our lives.

I call this a life of "coerced conformity" in which we are taught to sit still like robots, raise our hands to ask permission to take a leak, and be medicated if we are bored with the process or unable or unwilling to conform.

Peter Thiel, co-founder of PayPal and a billionaire investor and venture capitalist, writes of this conformity in an article published for the *Institute for Intercollegiate Studies*.

"In my teenage years and in my twenties, my path was insanely tracked. In my eighth-grade yearbook, one of my friends wrote, 'I know you're going to make it to Stanford in four years,'" writes Thiel. "I got into Stanford four years later. Then I went to Stanford Law School. I ended up at a big law firm in Manhattan."

Following that track, however, didn't bring the promised results.

"The firm was a place that from the outside everyone wanted to get into; on the inside it was a place that everybody wanted to leave," he writes. "When I left—after seven months and three days—one of the lawyers down the hall from me said, 'You know, I had no idea it was possible to escape from Alcatraz.'"

Why did the path he had followed since his youth—a path recommended by people who supposedly had his best interests at heart—lead to "Alcatraz"?

"The real problem is conformity, a fear of stepping outside the bounds," Thiel writes. "This is the issue I had to confront in myself when, after years of competing, I achieved my goal of working at a major law firm—and realized it was the last thing I wanted."

His comments shouldn't shock anyone.

After all, when Thomas Edison was seven years old, his schoolteacher belittled him for having an "addled" brain. Edison's mother pulled him out of school, and the young inventor was homeschooled for most of the rest of his education.

These days, society doesn't used the word "addled"—some might prefer ADHD. In his book *Free to Learn*, psychologist Peter Gray points out that as many as 12 percent of our kids are prescribed drugs due to being labeled ADHD. In most cases, Gray writes, it was based on complaints by their schoolteachers, most likely for "acting out" or talking in class—or perhaps for being more interested and passionate about some subjects than others.

So is it any surprise that people will stifle their desperation, forging ahead in a life that doesn't fulfill them, with days filled with things and activities they feel compelled to do rather than the things they actually want to do?

Living the Freedom Lifestyle means you do what you want, when you want, how you want—within the bounds of ethics, morality, and nonaggression against your fellow human beings.

A life of want. Not a life of compulsion.

2—MY HEALTH AND FITNESS ARE EXCELLENT

How much exercise do you get each day? What do you eat for your meals? Do you get at least eight hours of sleep per night? Are your meals full of sugar, grains, and other poisons?

Those are just a few questions to begin asking yourself.

We already met Tofe Evans, whose life of partying, drugs, and alcohol had left him a physical and mental mess. He's now doing ultramarathons at the blink of an eye.

We also met Fraser Cameron, a former world-class sprinter who fell into a life of grind and weight gain. Since he quit his job and made his transformation, he's back in top shape and training to compete in the master's track and field world championships.

When I was in high school, I ran track and cross country, after having played football my freshman year. During that year, despite being only five foot four and about 135 pounds, I had the strongest bench press and squat on the entire team. I ran the 5k in sixteen minutes flat and had a 4.6-second forty-yard dash. Not world-beating times, but I was in pretty damn good shape.

Entering college, I was 140 pounds, able to hammer out fifteen-mile runs with ease and planning to join the University of Iowa cross-country team as a walk-on. When I got to Iowa City, however, I discovered beer and the all-you-can-eat buffet in the student cafeteria. By the time spring break rolled around, I was 205 pounds. Yep, a sixty-five-pound weight gain.

That continued for three years, until I rediscovered my love of running during my senior year. That continued for several years after college, with me completing the Chicago Half Marathon in 1999. I was in great shape when my wife and I married in 2002, but then I fell back in a series of jobs that had me grinding.

In the year 2000, I had discovered that my cholesterol was high (more than 300), so the doctor recommended I take Lipitor. I began gaining weight again in 2002, and that unhealthiness continued until 2009. The entire time, I remained on Lipitor.

It was then that the anxiety attacks with corresponding stomach pains began to really take their toll. After an early morning trip to urgent care due to the pain, a doctor told me I probably had irritable bowel syndrome and prescribed a drug to help it.

He didn't tell me about the side effects of this particular drug, which left me with nervousness, extreme thirst, and an increased body temperature. It actually made me feel like I was going crazy, so I stopped taking it.

Shortly thereafter, I came upon a guest blog post in Tim Ferriss's *4-Hour Blog* by Robb Wolf, author of *The Paleo Solution*. Wolf wrote about many of the same symptoms I had been experiencing and pinpointed many of the same foods I was eating. In short, I was consuming a lot of grains and a lot of dairy.

Wolf advocates for the Paleo lifestyle. As the Mayo Clinic describes it, the Paleo diet is "based on foods similar to what might have been eaten during the Paleolithic era, which dates from approximately 2.5 million to 10,000 years ago" and "typically includes lean meats, fish, fruits, vegetables, nuts, and seeds—foods that in the past could be obtained by hunting and gathering."

Inspired by Wolf's blog post, I went Paleo the very next day. Almost ten years later, I'm in the best shape of my life. I stopped using Lipitor in 2009, and two years ago, my physician told me I had the best good-to-bad cholesterol ratio he had ever seen in a male my age.

As you can tell, I'm a big advocate for the Paleo or "primal" lifestyle. Do I recommend it? Absolutely. But how about starting with daily morning walks? Cutting grains and processed foods from your diet. Consuming fewer high-carbohydrate foods and more protein.

If your body isn't at 100 percent, you're not going to be able to be at 100 percent at work and with the people you love. My poor physical health no doubt contributed to my anxiety attacks and made me feel like I was trapped in a prison of weakness.

So if your health and fitness aren't excellent, you are not living the Freedom Lifestyle.

3—MY RELATIONSHIP WITH MY SPOUSE/ PARTNER IS EXCELLENT

My client, Steve (I've changed the name to protect his privacy), had a great job at a prestigious law firm. Having always been overweight, he had lost significant weight and got in great running shape.

His newfound confidence, however, got him into some trouble. He cheated on his wife the same week she announced to him that she was pregnant.

Yeah.

What he gained in health freedom he lost in relationship freedom. He almost lost his wife as well. His guilt plunged him into a life of gluttony and alcoholism. He told me stories of downing a gallon or two of Jack Daniels each week. He gained 150 pounds.

I worked with Steve to clearly define his life's vision and begin setting clear yearly, monthly, weekly, and daily outcomes to work toward that vision. He's lost the weight and improved his relationship with his wife.

Steve learned the hard way that our physical and mental health and our relationships are tied together.

One of my clients was being held back from shutting down his business to pursue an investment in a passion project because he was afraid his wife, a physician, would harbor ill will because she was the "breadwinner."

"Has she actually said this to you?" I asked him.

"Well, no. Not so much. But I can tell," he replied.

"I think you really should sit down and have a talk with her," I said.

So he did, and it turns out she wasn't harboring those feelings at all. They had been communicating in passive-aggressive quips and remarks, and as a result, assigning motives and feelings to one another that didn't actually exist.

Another one of my clients really wanted to move from her Midwestern city to a warmer southern city. She was absolutely certain her husband, however, did not want to move.

"The other day, we were at the park, and it was getting cold, and I complained," she told me. "So my husband said, 'Don't tell me, you really want to escape these winters and move to Charlotte.'"

And that was the end of their conversation. They were communicating by passive-aggressive quips. I urged her to have a heartfelt, honest conversation with her husband to let him know that she really did, in fact, want to move to Charlotte. Perhaps he didn't really know how strongly she felt.

It was also possible that he really had strong feelings against Charlotte but would be happy to move to a different southern city. The problem was, neither of them would ever know one another's true feelings unless they had a truly honest discussion.

Upon my last discussion with this former client, she

still hadn't—due to fear—had that discussion with her husband. I assume she is still trapped living in a city she doesn't like, never knowing what her husband would've said if she had just been honest with him.

You will never have true freedom unless your relationship with your spouse or partner is excellent.

4—I SPEND ENOUGH TIME INVESTING IN MYSELF

There are people who will spend $1,500 on a new TV or purchase a car they can't afford but refuse to spend nineteen dollars a month to join a gym, invest in visits to their doctor, or (selfishly, I'll add) hire a coach.

It's not just that self-care is the last thing we want to invest in; it's that we usually invest in things we want rather than things we need.

It's simple human nature.

A potential client once told me he couldn't join my course because he and his wife didn't want to add any additional debt to their credit card. This is right after he told me he had purchased a BMW and was looking forward to a week in Las Vegas with the guys.

Wants versus needs.

Another potential client told me he "just couldn't afford" my coaching course shortly after telling me what a wonderful weekend getaway he and his wife had in Gettysburg.

People readily invest in things they want. They hold off on things they need.

I've had moms tell me of their tremendous guilt at the mere thought of taking more time to invest in themselves for fear it would take away time invested in the family. Likewise, I've had men talk of their guilt over having to invest less time in work so they can invest in themselves.

The simple truth, however, is that if you don't invest in yourself, you won't be at 100 percent. If you're not at 100 percent, you can't possibly be at your optimum for your relationships or your work.

We've already looked at the importance of your mental and physical health and nutrition.

Investing in your overall self-care is a vital part of living the Freedom Lifestyle.

5—I'M FULFILLED EVERY SINGLE DAY, NOT JUST NIGHTS AND WEEKENDS

"Everybody's working for the weekend."

—LOVERBOY

There is a classic *Saturday Night Live* sketch from 1990 in which the very buff Patrick Swayze is competing with the decidedly nonbuff Chris Farley for a spot on the male shirtless Chippendales squad. The two are dancing to the 1981 Loverboy song referenced above, "Working for the Weekend."

"Everybody's working for the weekend/Everybody wants a little romance," goes the song. "Everybody's going off the deep end/Everybody needs a second chance."

I bring up the sketch in association with this song because I think they combine to create a metaphor that goes well beyond a simple "fat joke" sketch.

Swayze represents the life we wish we could live. Healthy. Good-looking. Great dance moves. Graceful.

Farley, on the other hand, represents how we often feel. Out of shape. Grinding away. Self-conscious.

Add in the Loverboy song, and you have a more complete picture: trudging through the week, in poor health, grinding away, and wishing you were living someone else's life. Living for nights and weekends because your days are filled with drudgery and quiet desperation.

Five years after that sketch, the movie *Office Space* was released. Popular because its humor reflected reality for many people stuck in unfulfilling careers, it features a now classic quote uttered by a female office worker to the main character, Peter Gibbons, when he appears frustrated and downtrodden on a Monday morning.

"Uh-oh. It looks like somebody's got a case of the Mondays," she says.

For far too many people, "a case of the Mondays" happens on a weekly basis. They wake up anxious Monday after Monday, with a tightness in their chest and a feeling of dread. One client told me her biggest challenge was just getting out of bed every Monday through Friday because she had to go in to a job that fundamentally left her unfulfilled.

In many cases, your Monday ruins your Saturday and Sunday. You come home from work on a Friday evening, plop down on your couch or head out with friends, and decompress. When you wake up on Saturday morning, however, you already begin thinking about Monday. Those thoughts prevent you from being fully present throughout the weekend. Even though you're at the zoo or the park with your family, your mind is elsewhere, thinking about that Monday morning staff meeting, the project left unfinished, the morning commute.

"I fucking hate Friday. I really do," writes marketing/ personal development guru Gary Vaynerchuk in a 2017 blog post. "I'm blown away by people celebrating the end of the week. Like the weekend is your escape from your reality. At its basic form, if you genuinely celebrate Friday, you need to rethink your entire fucking game. You need to rethink life."

Gary is correct. If you regularly suffer from a "case of the Mondays" and live for nights and weekends, something is broken. Something in your life is out of alignment.

There is no reason you shouldn't be fulfilled every day of the week. The choice is up to you.

Because only living for nights and weekends is certainly not part of the Freedom Lifestyle.

6—MY FAMILY AND I HAVE TRAVELED TO AT LEAST ONE PLACE WE REALLY WANTED TO GO (NOT HAVE TO GO FOR WORK OR EXTENDED FAMILY) IN THE PAST YEAR

"She said yes!"

The gondola driver shouted it out as the tears formed in my wife-to-be's eyes, and I heard applause erupt behind me. Down on one knee, I had just asked my wife to marry me on a gondola ride in the Grand Canal at the Venetian Resort and Casino in Las Vegas.

The interior of that resort is designed as an incredible replica of Venice, complete with its own Grand Canal, foot bridges, trattorias, gelaterias, piazzas, and singing gondoliers.

We were in Las Vegas on a long-planned trip with friends. A few weeks prior to the trip, I began to formulate my plan to propose. I let my friend in on the plan, and he and his wife stored the engagement ring in their hotel-room safe. As we approached the gondola, I nervously tried to strategically place myself so that Julie would get on the gondola first, and quickly switched the ring box from one pocket to another so that she wouldn't see the curious bulge in my pocket.

Everything went according to plan, and the cheers I heard

were because a crowd had gathered at the turnaround point of the gondola ride, and they all had seen the entire proposal unfold.

It was amazing. Throughout the rest of the weekend, we were stopped by people throughout Las Vegas who had seen the proposal and wanted to congratulate us. We felt like celebrities.

And we vowed to visit the real Grand Canal the following year to reenact the proposal on the real deal.

But my business got in the way. I started a new job right after our wedding and cut our honeymoon in half to impress my new boss. Then I moved from job to job before starting my own agency. Too busy. Too much work travel. Then we had kids.

Though I was making seven figures, we kept telling ourselves we'd travel to Venice when we just saved that "extra $5,000." We never seemed to have enough in the bank to warrant taking that trip.

Then I shut down my agency and went full time into coaching. My mindset shifted. Entering 2017, Julie and I decided that we'd finally take that trip. Not just a short trip to Venice but a five-week European trip through the UK, France, and Italy. In August, we took that trip, and seventeen years after my marriage proposal, we finally experienced that ride on the real Grand Canal—this time with our four kids.

It was just one incredible moment from our extended journey.

Touring the hallowed halls of Westminster Abbey. Getting an up-close look at the *Mona Lisa* at the Louvre. Sipping wine with Fraser Cameron and his family outside of Château de Fontainebleau. Hiking the ravine and exploring the caves underneath Gravina in Puglia, Italy, the town where my grandfather was born.

It was a trip like no other, and it fundamentally changed our lives, bringing our family closer together and expanding our frames of reference of what is possible. We're currently planning next year's trip, most likely to Scandinavia, and have already discussed trips for several years into the future.

The only bittersweet feeling is that we had delayed our European trip for so long. What if we had become ill or died during the previous seventeen years? We never would've been able to make the trip.

Believe it or not, money can be renewed, but time cannot because it is a nonrenewable resource.

If you continue to put off that trip you've always desired, you're not truly living the Freedom Lifestyle.

7—I HAVE A CLEARLY DEFINED VISION FOR MY LIFE

To save the world by helping individuals fight for lives of freedom and fulfillment.

That is my vision statement for my life. It combines my purpose for living with the impact I want to make on the world. It doesn't just apply to my work; it applies to my relationships and me. Whether it's how I live my life, how we raise our kids, how I build my business, or how I coach my clients, my vision statement provides a guiding star—that destination on a map where I want to end up.

We discuss vision statements in greater detail later in this book, but just know that it's something many people think they've defined but haven't.

People often ask me if they should have multiple vision statements throughout their life that change with their circumstances. The answer to that is no.

People often go through life thinking they need a series of vision statements. When you're in your twenties, you might think it's "Making partner at the firm and getting a

$100,000 salary." When you're in your thirties, it might be "Finding my spouse and having kids."

These aren't vision statements. They're temporary objectives. And when people spend their lives going from objective to objective with no real vision statement that connects those objectives, they arrive at their forties or fifties feeling lost.

Your vision statement should be your rock. The outcome you want for your life. Then you should create yearly objectives that all lead toward that rock. Then monthly, weekly, and daily objectives that lead toward those yearly objectives.

Should your objectives change? Absolutely. There are always multiple ways to get to any destination. Your strengths, your challenges, your life circumstances will regularly force you to stop, pivot, and try new routes.

But your vision statement is that end destination. Whether you die one hour from now or twenty years from now, where do you want to be?

8—MY SPOUSE AND I HAVE AT LEAST TWO DATE NIGHTS PER MONTH

But, Curt, we already spoke about relationships.

Yes, and I'm highlighting them again because relationships are the most important thing in our lives.

"Our relationships and how happy we are in our relationships have a powerful influence on our health," Dr. Robert Waldinger told the *Harvard Gazette* in a 2017 interview. "Taking care of your body is important, but tending to your relationships is a form of self-care too."

Waldinger is a professor of psychiatry at Harvard Medical School and a psychiatrist at Massachusetts General Hospital.

He also is the director of the eighty-plus-year Harvard Study of Adult Development, which has followed the lives of 724 men since 1938. Researchers have followed up with each of the men annually, asking them about their work, families, and themselves.

What lessons are to be learned from this long-running study?

"Well, the lessons aren't about wealth or fame or working harder and harder," explained Waldinger in his November 2015 TED Talk. "The clearest message that we get from this seventy-five-year study is this: good relationships keep us happier and healthier. Period."

He explained that when most of the men in the study were just starting out, they thought that "fame, wealth, and high achievement" were going to be the keys to a happy life. That turned out not to be the case.

"It wasn't their middle-age cholesterol levels that predicted how they were going to grow old," revealed Waldinger. "It was how satisfied they were in their relationships," he concluded.

Strong relationships also appear to keep us physically and mentally strong.

"The people who were the most satisfied in their relationships at age fifty were the healthiest at age eighty. And good, close relationships seem to buffer us from some of the slings and arrows of getting old," said Waldinger. "Our most happily partnered men and women reported, in their eighties, that on the days when they had more physical pain, their mood stayed just as happy. But the people who were in unhappy relationships, on the days when they reported more physical pain, it was magnified by more emotional pain."

So yes, I mention relationships twice in my Freedom Index because they are so damn important.

"Are you kidding me? Dates nights two times a month? I

wish!" commented one woman in response to a LinkedIn post I published about the Freedom Index. "Not with two in college and one in a private school, but I love the thought. Does checking out free movies from the local library count?"

Around the same time, one of my clients told me he and his wife really didn't like "date nights" because they felt forced and usually meant spending too much money on an expensive meal.

Who says "date night" has to be expensive? Or at a restaurant? Or an event at night, for that matter?

My wife and I have had some of our best dates while eating lunch at Chipotle or walking on the beach or checking out a movie.

Your date night could involve dinner at home with some nice music and candles.

Focus on the outcome, not the input. The outcome is that you want to have uninterrupted time with your significant other to enjoy their company and really communicate with each other.

Stop looking for excuses, and just make it happen. Otherwise, you're not truly living the Freedom Lifestyle.

9—I LOVE MY JOB AND IT FULFILLS ME

According to the World Bank, the average lifespan for someone living in the United States is a little more than seventy-eight years. That equates to 683,280 hours in the average lifespan.

Jessica Pryce-Jones, author of *Happiness at Work*, estimates we spend an average of ninety thousand hours at work during our lifetimes. That's around 13 percent of our total lifespan spent at work.

What if we subtract the nonworking years of our lives (roughly ages 1–21 and ages 66–78) from the average lifespan? It turns out we spend about 23 percent of our total adult lives at work.

Taking this further, what if we only account for our waking hours? A 2013 Gallup study found the average American only gets 6.8 hours of sleep per night. That leaves 282,510 waking hours over the course of our forty-five-year work life, which means more than 31 percent of our lives are spent working.

That's on average. There are those who work much more, who spend twelve to fourteen extra hours per week at the office. And that doesn't take into account the hours we spend worrying about work during nights and weekends.

So if you're spending almost one-third of your life at work, why wouldn't you want—demand—that your work be fulfilling? Why are you spending such a large portion of your waking hours on something you don't love?

It's easy to conjure thoughts of your father or grandfather toiling away in a coal mine or in a hard-labor job during the Great Depression. Those thoughts can foster guilt. Remember my earlier section on using gratitude as an excuse not to want more in your life?

"Hey, it's a job, and that's what's important," a friend once told me when I told him I was bored with my first job out of college.

That's what we were taught by our parents. That's the mindset we carry into adulthood. It's the shackles we put on ourselves to justify our comfort zone of misery, in which we are spending one-third of our lives in a job that leaves us with the "blahs" or, worse yet, sucks our soul.

You deserve better, and if you're not in a job you love, a job that fulfills you, then you're not living the Freedom Lifestyle.

10—MY WORK, FAMILY, AND SELF ARE IN PERFECT ALIGNMENT

If you're someone who is chasing the mythical "work-life balance," I have news for you: it doesn't exist. I challenge you to wipe your vocabulary clean of that term because it's bullshit.

The fundamental problem is that we are taught to think of work and life as two separate things. Really?

There's not work *and* life; there's just life. How you spend the time in your life is entirely up to you. The key to freedom and fulfillment isn't balance; it's alignment: aligning the three facets in your life—work, family, and self.

Alignment is explored more deeply in a later chapter, but let's just review what we've already seen in terms of the various pieces of your life fitting together.

Dr. Waldinger's study showed the interconnectedness of relationships on your mental and physical health. The stories I've shared about Tofe, Steve, Fraser, Eric, and myself clearly show how our work, family, and self all rely on one another to keep our lives running at full throttle.

The way many people look at "work-life balance" is this: they keep their heads down in misery, hoping that in a week, everything will ease up, and they'll restore balance by spending more time with their family.

Often, that week turns into a month, which turns into a year, which turns into a decade, which turns into the voice in their head saying, When I get to sixty-five, I'll retire, we'll travel the world, and it will all balance out.

Aside from the fact that this means you'll spend the peak physical years of your life in constant toil, it ignores the fact that there is no guarantee you or the people you love will make it to sixty-five years old. I've known many people who made it to sixty-five only to have a heart attack or see their spouse stricken with cancer or have their knee go out or suffer some physical or mental breakdown that prevented them from restoring the balance as planned.

Alignment takes this into account and focuses on getting the three facets of your life to begin working in harmony *now* in a way that works for you and you alone.

If you're seeking balance instead of alignment, you're not living the Freedom Lifestyle.

CHAPTER 3

ABUNDANCE VS. SCARCITY

In early January 2017, Julie, the kids, and I headed out to California for a two-week vacation that took us from La Jolla to Hollywood to the Hearst Castle to Yosemite to San Francisco.

While we were in La Jolla, which is just outside of San Diego, we decided to spend a day in the local wine country of the Temecula Valley. After visiting several wineries, we stopped at Lorenzi Winery, which was founded by Don Lorenzi, a local magazine publisher.

Speaking with the server in the tasting room about Lorenzi's story as I sipped some of his bold reds, I began to think long and hard about why I couldn't one day achieve one of my dreams: owning a winery.

A big goal? Absolutely. But I believe your objectives

should be so big and audacious that they make you feel uncomfortable. They should actually make you feel a little embarrassed to tell other people.

We left the winery, and that night, I attended a local networking event. But I could not get the thought of owning my own winery out of my head. It was the last thought I had before drifting off to sleep and the first thought in my head when I woke up.

Driving from La Jolla up to Hollywood the next day, I pulled the car over and told Julie I was going to record a video for my followers on LinkedIn and Facebook. In that video, I shared my goal of owning a winery.

"I'm going to own a winery," I stated in the video. "Maybe not next year. Or the year after. But ten years from now? Why not?"

I explained the story of my trip to Lorenzi Vineyards and how I didn't have a doubt in my mind that my goal would one day become a reality.

"My abundance mindset caused me—forced me—to think: Why not me?" I said. "I can see it now: my family name on the bottle. Producing a big, red cab, just as dry and musty as I like it. Leaving a legacy to pass down to future generations."

I continued to draw a line in the sand.

"If I had a scarcity mindset, I would've thought, That's out of reach," I explained. "Do you have an abundance mindset or a scarcity mindset? If your mindset is one of scarcity, you'll never break out of the rut you find yourself in today."

The abundance versus scarcity theme is one I had been considering for a while, but this was the first time I decided to address it. I have to admit I was feeling it.

After all, the very California trip we were taking would've previously been considered "too expensive" by us—even when I was bringing in significantly more revenue from my agency. The trip was actually taking place at the same time I would normally have been at a multiday meeting for one of my former clients.

Instead of having to sit through that meeting, I was tasting wine and conjuring dreams of one day making my own.

So what's the difference between an abundance mindset and a scarcity mindset?

My friend Mike Johnson described "abundance" best when he commented on LinkedIn in response to my winery video.

"Visualizing and feeling as if the achievement is already attained speeds its manifestation," wrote Mike, a former journalist who is now an early retirement expert. (More on Mike later in this chapter.) You already have it, just live from that assumption until present time sucks that future to today."

What about scarcity? Austin H. exemplified it well when he wrote on Facebook in response to my video, "This dude is never going to own a winery."

Stephen Covey popularized—hell, he may even have coined—the term "abundance mentality" in his best-selling 1989 book, *The Seven Habits of Highly Effective People.* Covey describes it as "a concept in which a person believes there are enough resources and successes to share with others."

I would go further than Covey to say an abundance mindset is one that looks at something that seems impossible and says, "Why not?"

Per his definition, however, it also applies to people who achieved success and said, "Why not me?"

Covey goes on to write that "most people are deeply scripted in what I call the Scarcity Mentality.

"They see life as having only so much, as though there

were only one pie out there," he writes. "And if someone were to get a big piece of the pie, it would mean less for everybody else."

This mentality was on display later in the year, in September 2017, when I posted a video from the beach.

You see, I set a limit for myself of only working twelve hours per week. The rest of my time is filled with activities and things that fulfill me: time with the kids, working out, reading, dates with my wife, etc.

We homeschool our kids, with my wife doing the great majority of the schooling work. As such, one day per week, I take the kids and my wife has a day off—she can go out and do whatever she wants. On those days, sometimes I take the kids to a museum, sometimes I take them to the park, and sometimes I take them to the beach.

On one September Wednesday, we went to the beach. I decided to film a video where I spoke of my "twelve-hour work limit" and the fact that I had built a lifestyle in which I can go to the beach with my kids on a weekday.

"How did this nonsense end up on LinkedIn?" asked one commenter in response to my beach video. "Twelve hours of work a week? What's the wife doing all day? Waiting at the beach? And the kids? No school, no activities?"

"You must've inherited your money," asserted another commenter.

"He must've married rich," wrote yet another.

Those comments clearly represent the scarcity mindset: being so trapped by your limiting beliefs that you can't even believe someone else would be able to actually design their lifestyle.

It's that type of mindset that can fill you with jealousy rather than motivation when you look at other successful people.

It's that type of mindset that resigns you to a life of mediocrity instead of a life of abundance.

And it's that type of mindset that keeps you trapped in the life of quiet desperation we discussed in Chapter 1 of this book.

The first step to living a life of freedom and fulfillment is blowing apart that scarcity mindset and adopting one of abundance.

GRATITUDE AND ACHIEVEMENT

After day one of my retreat ended and we were walking

toward the restaurant for our group dinner, one of my clients asked me if we were going to discuss how to achieve an abundance mindset the next day. I told him to hold that thought.

On the morning of day two of the retreat, we recapped everything we had done and discussed on day one. We had discussed a number of short, simple activities that, when done every day, will lead up to an abundance mindset.

An abundance mindset doesn't just happen. You don't just flip a switch and create it. If you've had a scarcity mindset for years, it's damn difficult to make the switch. Just like anything, it takes small steps, accomplished every day, to make change happen.

The first activity I introduced was one that was drilled into me by my coach, the previously mentioned Fraser Cameron. It's an activity I've read and heard about but which I had never done consistently until Fraser held me accountable.

The activity involves instilling a daily dose of gratitude and achievement in your life.

Grab a small notebook that will be dedicated solely for the purpose of this activity. I tend to love my Moleskin notebooks, but use whatever works for you. Make sure that notebook is on the nightstand by your bed at all times.

Every night, right before you go to bed, think about three things you're truly grateful for. Be honest and thoughtful. Try not to repeat people, activities, or things more than once in a month. For example, I'm grateful for my wife and kids every single day. It would be easy for me to write them in my notebook on a daily basis. But that defeats the purpose of this activity.

The goal is to begin looking for the variety of things in your life you can and should be grateful for. There are the obvious things, such as the roof over your head, the food on your table, the clothes on your back, and the people you love.

When I began doing this activity on a daily basis, however, I began to look for new things to be grateful for. Perhaps it was seeing the dozen wild turkeys roaming our neighborhood on my morning walk. It might be the out-of-the-blue hug my four-year-old son gave me as I walked in the door. It could even be a particularly nice comment someone made to me throughout the course of the day.

Think of three things. Write them down. Every night. Right before you go to bed.

Then write down three outcomes you achieved that day. Don't just write down "tasks" or "to-dos" that you crossed off that day. We're going to talk about becoming radically outcomes-focused later in this book, but for now, just know that key outcomes are those things that move you toward your life vision. The three things that helped you win the day—whether it be in your work, with your family, or involving you.

Think of three achievements. Write them down. Every night. Right before you go to bed.

When you wake up each morning, don't check your smartphone. Don't look at your tablet. Pick up your notebook instead and review what you wrote down the night before. This way, you're beginning and ending every single day with a dose of gratitude and achievement.

After several weeks of doing this, you'll condition your mind to begin looking for the good in the world. You'll also start acting to build your days around gratitude and focusing on key outcomes to achieve. Your mindset will improve. By achieving key outcomes each day, you'll build every day toward bigger objectives, and you'll realize what's possible.

All of this moves you in the direction of an abundance mindset. You'll start asking, "Why not?" instead of saying,

"I can't." You'll begin looking at the success of others as motivation to reach for more yourself while also being happy with the gifts you currently have in your life.

WHAT'S AWESOME ABOUT TODAY?

No matter what we do, some mornings are just going to be worse than others. We can reduce the amount of things we hate in our day, but there are always going to be days when we have to do things that suck. The gratitude and achievement activities can certainly help.

But let's also think about the conversations we have in our own heads when we wake up in the morning (or throughout the day, for that matter).

Have you ever woken up and thought, *Crap, I have to talk to that so-and-so client today?*

Or *Ugh, I just don't feel like going to that networking event.*

Those conversations in our heads set the tone for the day. They determine whether we are going to have an abundant day—or a day filled with scarcity.

Instead of having those negative conversations, simply ask yourself these three questions:

- What's awesome about today?
- What could I choose to do to make it even more awesome?
- How am I going to make those things happen?

Three simple questions that can flip the script for how you want to live the day.

First, every single day is awesome. Perhaps you're waking up next to someone you love, or you're going to see people you love during the course of the day. The sun is shining. You have a bed to sleep in and a roof over your head. You're above ground instead of six feet under.

Whatever your reasons for the day being awesome, they are there. I guarantee it.

The second question not only forces you to think of additional things you could add into this already awesome day, but it stresses the fact that how you spend the time in your life is entirely up to you.

Perhaps that networking event you dread yet attend weekly isn't providing you with your desired outcomes. You keep going, however, because you feel compelled to do it. The awesome thing you could add to your day is the decision to stop attending the event. Remember—part of living the Freedom Lifestyle is spending your days doing things you want instead of things you feel compelled to do.

On the other hand, maybe the networking event is producing your desired outcomes, but you still dread attending. Choose to stop at your favorite store, coffee shop, bar, or restaurant on the drive back from the event. Add something you love to the event to make it even a little more awesome.

You can choose to do this. You deserve to choose to do this.

Instead of just thinking this in your head, get up and write down your concrete plan (in your paper calendar, smartphone calendar, wall calendar, whatever) to make your plan for increased awesomeness happen. If you decide to stop attending the weekly networking event, get up right there and then and email the organizers, telling them you're stepping down. Or get up and block off your calendar an hour or two after the event so you can stop at your favorite store or restaurant.

Identify what's already awesome in your day.

Think about what can make it more awesome.

Put together the plan to make it happen.

Paired with the gratitude and achievement activity, your mindset will be further bolstered, and abundance will soon drown out the thoughts of scarcity that have been plaguing you for years.

STOP ASKING FOR PERMISSION

We live in a permission-based society. Ever since we were young, we've been conditioned to ask for permission.

Permission to go to the bathroom. Permission to speak. Permission to go play with the neighbor kids. Permission to get a driver's license. Permission to major in the college subject we desire. Permission to take vacation. Permission to come into the office late.

Permission to...well, you get the idea.

It's no surprise, then, that even when we get to adulthood, we're conditioned to feel like we need to ask permission to live the lifestyle we desire.

Take, for example, my former client Brian. He joined one of my group courses because he said he needed to find his life purpose. He was not entirely happy with his career, he was on his second marriage, and he said he couldn't shake the feeling that he was "destined for more."

He signed up for my course, did some of the early calls, but then got stymied when I asked four simple questions:

- What do you like to do?
- What do you love to do?
- What do you hate to do?
- If you had a magic wand and could magically transport yourself into your desired lifestyle, what would it look like?

Not only had Brian never even considered those questions, he honestly felt he needed permission to even consider answering them. He was so trapped in the prison of his permission mindset that he was simply unable to define his desired lifestyle, much less live it.

Brian's story is one I've seen time and again. And it's one that exemplifies how my life used to be.

I once thought I needed permission to live the life I wanted. Permission from whom? I have no idea. And that's the point. The only person you need permission from to start living a life of freedom and fulfillment is... you.

Forget the expectations of others. Forget your past. Forget your bad habits. Give yourself permission to define and live the lifestyle you want.

Earlier in this book, I mentioned a client who desperately wanted to move to a warmer southern climate but was afraid her husband didn't share her desire. That wasn't the only thing holding her back. She and her husband both felt they needed permission to move to a new city when their only reason was simple desire rather than having to move for a new job. She told me in the South American country where they were born and raised that was simply unheard of.

You need a job—or some other good reason—to pick up and move to a new city. And simply wanting to doesn't count as a good enough reason.

Says who? Exactly.

Perhaps we feel we need permission from our parents (even when we're well into our forties). Maybe we think we need permission from our significant others (even though we're afraid to have honest, candid discussions with them). It could be we think we need the permission of society, which is known to look askance at people who decide to lead lifestyles that veer outside the bounds of conformity.

I'm no longer amazed at otherwise mild-mannered people—people who never express their opinions on religion or politics—who will go out of their way to express their displeasure at the fact my wife and I homeschool our kids. Don't we need the permission of the government to do that? That, along with additional queries, is at the root of their concerns.

Everyone seems to feel they need permission.

Isaac Morehouse is someone who has experienced the permission mindset firsthand. Like me, he spent many years in a career in politics and public policy but left it to start a for-profit company, Praxis, that offers apprenticeships with startups as an alternative to college.

With a 98 percent placement rate in jobs that average $50,000–60,000 per year starting salary, Praxis puts attendees through a six-month bootcamp, after which time they compete to get hired by startup companies around the country. They pay $11,000 to enter the program, but then are paid $14,000 by the companies during their apprenticeship.

In other words, instead of racking up hundreds of thousands in debt from attending a college or university, they get paid to gain real-world skills and enter the workforce ready to roll and without debt.

It seems like a no-brainer, except for the fact that many parents have spent years cultivating a mindset that their kids absolutely, positively must earn a college degree. Never mind whether that degree will lead to an actual job, much less a fulfilling career.

Isaac told me that despite the thousands of applications they get each year, many applicants bow out due to pressure from their parents. Despite being eighteen-year-old adults, they feel they need the permission of their parents to veer outside the lines of conformity—and their parents simply won't give it, even though the student could always go back to college at a later date.

For this reason, the simple advice I always offer to eighteen-year-olds is this: think for yourself.

Hug and kiss your parents, and thank them for everything they've done for you to this point. Listen to their advice and to the advice of those around you. But then chart your own path.

Don't spend hundreds of thousands of dollars going to college for four years to "find yourself." There are less expensive and more effective ways to do that. If you want to be a brain surgeon or a nuclear physicist, then of course you'll need a degree. But four years to get a degree in marketing? It makes no sense.

So many people spend their lives and dollars chasing

other people's expectations or opinions. Then they get to their forties and fifties and wish they had paved their own way when they were younger. They still feel they need permission to live the life they desire. A permission-based mindset leads to a scarcity mindset, and it will hold you back.

Whether you're eighteen or fifty, it's time to stop asking permission.

BE A SEEKER AND A PEEKER

"I'm trying to create seekers and peekers, not moaners and groaners," said Don Wettrick, the founder of Start-EdUp Innovation, LLC, and StartEdUp Foundation, both based in Indianapolis, Indiana.

Wettrick, whose father was a public schoolteacher, spent most of his career as a teacher as well. He created an innovative program at Noblesville High School in Noblesville, Indiana, which resembles more of startup incubator than a high school classroom—and has a popular podcast, *StartEDUp*, through which he has interviewed the likes of Gary Vaynerchuk and Seth Godin and yours truly.

When I interviewed Don on my podcast, he explained the difference between "seekers and peekers" and "moaners and groaners." The latter complain, while the former see opportunities everywhere.

Seekers and peekers are always learning and always adapting.

"If you're like, 'I'm going to go out there and find what's next,' then you can own it," said Wettrick. "And those are the people who are free. Their options are available. They're not really tied to one thing. They're like water. I mean, honestly, what it usually boils down to is the mindset, you know: Are you looking for opportunities, or are you complaining?"

Mike Johnson is someone who has made his career out of profiting off of opportunities. A former newspaperman from Florida, he moved with his wife to Cody, Wyoming, the former home of the legendary Buffalo Bill Cody. There they started a profitable trolley tour company. He later became an early retirement expert, making millions through ownership and management of mobile home parks, and now donates his time to help others do the same.

I had the pleasure of meeting Mike at a conference in February 2017, and of interviewing him on my podcast. It was a 2015 LinkedIn article he wrote, however, that blew me away and really demonstrated the power of being open to opportunities.

"Opportunity is everywhere," Johnson writes in his article "How I Turned a Folding Chair into $315,000." "You just have to ask, 'What's missing?' and 'How can I profitably provide that?'"

Mike explains that his trolley tour company was head-quartered in the Irma Hotel, which was apparently built by Buffalo Bill himself.

"Six nights a week, the hotel sponsored an Old West play that ended with a gunfight right in the street in front of the hotel," he writes. "It attracted over three hundred people per night. The show was free, but seating was limited to a few picnic tables and the curb. Most people had to stand for the forty-minute show. Operating on the porch as we did, we had a close look at customer discomfort. Many times we'd bring a few chairs out of the hotel for elderly viewers."

Those chairs turned into a profitable opportunity for Mike. As he explains, the show had been operating "for over fifty years without adequate seating, yet no one had done anything about it." So Mike rented a dozen folding chairs, put them out, and charged one dollar per chair for people to sit.

One of his employees told Mike it was the "dumbest idea" he'd ever heard of, but he changed his mind once Mike kept selling out his rented chairs. Year after year.

After twelve years, when Mike finally sold the business—including the chair-rental service—he estimates they had generated more than $315,000 in revenue just from the rented chairs.

Where others missed the opportunity, Mike profited. Where some thought it was a dumb idea, Mike didn't ask for permission.

Actively seeking opportunities is yet another key to cultivating an abundance mindset. And that is a vital part of living a life of freedom and fulfillment.

CHAPTER 4

IT TAKES MORE THAN FREEDOM

"It ain't over yet."

Those were the last words my father said to me. I can remember them so clearly.

The previous week was Thanksgiving, and my wife and three kids (our youngest hadn't yet been born) were spending our first real vacation at our new part-time home in Charleston, South Carolina.

On Thanksgiving morning, my dad had shared the news with me that the doctor had declared him "cancer-free" earlier in the week. My dad had been fighting a combination of prostate and bladder cancer for several years. Two years earlier, the doctors had given him only four to six months to live.

My dad, however, was a fighter, and he gave it his all.

Now it appeared he had won the fight.

Two days later, on November 24, my dad and I texted back and forth as we watched our beloved Notre Dame Fighting Irish (my dad was a grad) defeat the University of South Carolina Trojans to go a perfect 12–0 on the year.

The morning after that win, my dad entered the hospital. Later that night, it began to look bleak as my father's kidneys—ravaged from years of radiation and chemo treatments—began to fail.

My mom kept me informed while my wife and I prepared for the drive back to the Chicago suburbs from Charleston. There was no rush. I was in denial.

There had been a number of similar-feeling false alarms during the previous two years. Furthermore, the doctor had just declared my dad cancer-free. Couldn't my dad just beat this latest challenge as well?

As we took the fifteen-hour drive home, the news got darker and darker. By the time I arrived at the hospital, they had begun the process of palliative care. Morphine to ease the pain while my dad slipped into heaven.

He was still semilucid when I approached his bed and held his hand. We talked about the big Notre Dame win.

"They did it," I declared.

"It ain't over yet," he replied.

Was he referring to the fact that the Fighting Irish still had to play the National Championship game versus Alabama? Yes.

But, to me, it meant more than that.

To me, it meant he wasn't done fighting. And he wasn't—holding on for another four days (we sat by his bed while he snored away in a morphine-induced sleep) until he passed away.

When I was asked to deliver the eulogy at his funeral, I chose to read from Dylan Thomas's timeless poem, "Do Not Go Gentle into That Good Night."

> Do not go gentle into that good night,
>
> Old age should burn and rave at close of day;
>
> Rage, rage against the dying of the light.

As I reflected on his final words, it struck me that my dad wasn't just talking about Notre Dame's season. His words were a call to action for me to fight for the freedom and fulfillment I lacked in my life.

Sure, I had built some freedom. During the past several years, I had significantly cut the number of hours I worked each day. With the help of the Gallup Strengths-Finder program, I had begun working in my "strengths zone" (more on that later), and so I was more efficient and productive.

The purchase of the vacation home in South Carolina was a big part of that freedom agenda.

As I wrote earlier, the words everyone spoke at my dad's funeral showed me it takes more than just freedom.

It also takes fulfillment.

LA DOLCE VITA

Having grown up in Trieste, Italy—just miles from what used to be the border with Communist Yugoslavia during the Tito regime—Paolo Ciccone has an appreciation for freedom.

"For me, freedom means the ability to create," he told

me. "We have a big brain here," he said, pointing to his forehead. "The frontal lobe here is all about imagining things."

He continued, "We often hear people saying, 'I'm a very visual person.' Well, we are all visual people. It is vital for us to create. You can write, you can paint, photograph, be involved in music, or use your creativity to build a new business."

As history has shown, he said, this freedom to create is one of the first things quashed when totalitarian regimes grab power.

"Think about this," he said. "In Soviet Russia, rock 'n' roll was illegal. In Afghanistan, the Taliban made TVs illegal. The first thing that a repressive regime does is to clamp down on creativity."

Why?

"Because they are afraid of it," he explained. "The freedom of creating, expressing yourself, is a disruptive force for good, and so I think that for me, freedom is definitely to be creative."

Paolo currently uses his freedom to create as the top personal branding photographer in Charleston, South

Carolina. His father was a photographer who spent years creating software as well as working in Hollywood on the sets of hit television shows such as *24*, *The Office*, and *The Unit*.

"He [my father] is the one who introduced me to photography," explained Paolo. "I went to the Art Institute, where I had been very involved with visual arts. I love music, I play a little bit of guitar. So throughout my life, when I was a software engineer, I was involved in another creative activity. Writing software is an incredibly creative and artistic activity."

He added, "All my life has been characterized by creation. It's something that excites me."

That desire to create is what brought him to the United States.

"In the very early 1980s, I got interested in computers," he explained. "It was the beginning of the PC revolution, and it really sparked my curiosity. I wanted to understand more about it, and in a couple of years, I became a software developer. Then a few more years passed, and in the early nineties I became sort of an expert on certain programs by a company called Borland. Borland used to make computer languages. We were actually building the languages that developers then used."

He loved the company, which helped him obtain his visa, which allowed him to move to the United States in 1994.

"I always liked the connection of technology and people," he said. "It's always the common thread—technology empowering people. I love that stuff. I wanted to be involved in that kind of field."

After several years, he said the company began going "downhill," so he left it to start an e-commerce company related to motorcycles.

Before long, however, he felt "that call to the artistic-visual part again."

So he became a cinematographer.

"I started doing some work with high-definition digital cameras back then, and I got a call to work on a program and on a TV pilot in LA," he said. "It was fantastic. I had to be on the stage on programs like 24. We were interviewing the people behind the camera—the people who make the show, cinematographers, gaffers, readers, people in special effects, lighting technicians."

He continued, "There is so much artistry that goes on in the show, and often, people are not aware."

Paolo called it a fantastic experience, and even though he had freedom in his life and was exercising it through a series of creative endeavors, there was still something missing.

"Well, I spent twenty-two years in California, and I was living in Santa Cruz, which is on the Central Coast," said Paolo. "I did my stint in LA, and after that, I thought, You know, this is a lot of fun, but I wanted to do something a little more meaningful than just being involved in pure entertainment."

He had freedom, but he wanted something with more meaning.

More fulfillment.

"I wanted to work with people," he said. "To be more involved directly in the lives of people, and after a lot of thinking and imagining and considering all that speculation, I thought, You know what? Photography. Photography is something I can handle on my own and have a more direct connection with people. Doing portrait photography allows me to be creative and provides meaning."

In 2016, he and his wife picked up and moved across the country to Charleston, South Carolina, where he has some family.

His journey from Trieste to California to South Carolina brought him freedom.

Now, he is experiencing a life of fulfillment as a personal branding photographer.

"It's exciting," he said. "You have to think on your feet. You have to take care of all of the technical parts related to the camera and connect with the person you're photographing because if there is no connection, nothing works, you know? So it has to be human. Has to be creative. That is the part that excites me."

It takes more than freedom.

It also takes fulfillment.

REDEFINING SUCCESS

Her blue glasses and no-BS style have garnered her millions of video views on LinkedIn and helped her become one of the Internet's most recognizable personal branding consultants.

To get to that point, however, Dr. Natalia Wiechowski had to travel a journey to understand just who she is.

As a girl of Polish descent growing up in Germany, Natalia

told me her authentic Germanness was often questioned while growing up.

Years later, she found herself working for some major corporations in Dubai in the United Arab Emirates. Outwardly, she was a success.

Internally, however, she wasn't so sure.

"People would tell me, 'Oh, Natalia, you made it,'" she explained to me while a guest on *The Freedom Club Podcast*.

"You're so successful. You're amazing. You're always positive," she said.

She was twenty-nine years old at the time and said she was highly confused. People perceived her as successful and very positive, but she was anything but.

"I was not happy. I was not successful. I was continuously sick. I was consuming like a crazy person," she said. "I was beating myself up emotionally to an extent where I literally ended up in hospital once, twice per month, and no doctor could find a solution."

This went on for a while, until Natalia decided to hit the "reset button" and take a break.

"This was the point where I realized, apparently, it's the right time to go on a sabbatical," she said, "forget everything I've ever learned, question everything that I've ever learned, and change the way I think, speak, act, eat, consume, change the people in my life, and start figuring out why I'm here on this planet."

She had money. She had financial freedom.

But she didn't have the fulfillment—that sense that you feel like you're doing what you were put on this earth to do.

"I didn't know where to start, and the whole thing scared the hell out of me because it meant that everything—the foundation, the values, the safe bubble that I'd created for myself—it was an illusion of control," she said. "And I had no clue in which direction to go. It was like Alice falling down the rabbit hole. It's just like, 'Ah, what's going on?'"

Like most people, Natalia needed the pain of the status quo to become greater than the pain of making a change. This process, she said, took six years.

"I think the first big massive moment where I realized, 'What on Earth am I doing with my life?' was the age of twenty-three," she explained. "And I changed a few things, but I didn't have the courage to really dig deeper and to figure out what it is that I want to do. At that stage, I was still thinking I want too much."

She said she continued to tell herself "nonsense lies" to distract herself from what she really wanted and instead lived a life she thought she "had to do because everybody else was doing it."

Once on her sabbatical, she says, the process of finding her purpose wasn't without pain.

"It was painful. It was messy, and it took forever because I did it on my own. I didn't ask for professional help," she explained. "So for me, it was literally, first of all, cleansing, detoxing. That was the first step."

"And then once I was somehow in the mindset of allowing new things...understanding that my dream job doesn't exist unless I create it, which was exciting but then again terrifying. So I just set the stage, just literally created a list with things that I always wanted to do, and I did them bit by bit."

HAPPINESS ISN'T FULFILLMENT

"How are you?" I asked Thomas Heath, a local personal branding coach in Charleston, South Carolina, and my cohost for our LinkedInLocal Charleston events series.

After giving it some thought, Thomas replied, "I'm going with fulfilled today."

Thomas had some illnesses in his family and additional stressors impacting him, but his response was much more accurate than a typical "Not so hot" or "Doing great!" response.

"You can be happy and fulfilled, or you can be sad and fulfilled," he explained to me. "Or you can be happy and unfulfilled or sad and unfulfilled."

Thomas was absolutely correct.

Happiness isn't the same as fulfillment, though I often see people use the terms interchangeably. Happiness can be fleeting, while fulfillment is something much deeper in our foundation.

For years, as I wrote previously, I lacked fulfillment in my life. I was missing that sense that I know why I'm here on this planet.

During those years, were there times when I was happy? Of course. I was happy when I was with my wife, kids, friends, family—and at many points in between.

But when those happy times faded, I was left alone with

my thoughts, with that underlying feeling that I was destined for more.

On the flip side, can you feel sad when you're fulfilled? Yep. Shit happens. People get sick. People die.

When you are fundamentally fulfilled, it's easier to leave the sad days behind—and to catapult yourself out of whatever rut you're in.

When you are fulfilled, you have a sense of meaning in your life.

"The pursuit of meaning—not happiness—is what makes life worthwhile," writes best-selling author Tom Rath in *Are You Fully Charged?* "People who spend life seeking happiness are unlikely to find it. Much like chasing fame or wealth, seeking happiness alone is misguided and can lead to poor decisions."

Dr. Jordan B. Peterson, professor of psychology at the University of Toronto, a clinical psychologist, and the author of the best seller *12 Rules for Life: An Antidote to Chaos,* forcefully makes the same argument.

In fact, his Rule 7—"Pursue what is meaningful (not what is expedient)"—centers around the pursuit of meaning, rather than mere happiness or pleasure.

"What is expedient works only for the moment," writes Peterson. "What is meaningful, by contrast, is the organization of what would otherwise merely be expedient into a symphony of Being. Meaning is what is put forth more powerfully than mere words can express by Beethoven's 'Ode to Joy,' a triumphant bringing forth from the void of pattern after pattern upon beautiful pattern, every instrument playing its part, disciplined voices layered on top of that, spanning the entire breadth of human emotion from despair to exhilaration."

On the other hand, he asserts, the pursuit of expedient pleasure and happiness has led to pain and suffering in the world.

Peterson points to the behaviors and mindset of criminals and tyrants.

"Pursue pleasure. Follow your impulses. Live for the moment. Do what's expedient. Lie, cheat, steal, deceive, manipulate—but don't get caught," he writes. "In an ultimately meaningless universe, what possible difference could it make?"

It is this striving for meaning instead of instant gratification—the sacrifice and delayed wait for meaning—that leads to good works and the triumph over pain and suffering.

That alleviation of pain and suffering is, in and of itself, a key plank of freedom, points out Dr. Bobby Koneru, a Dubuque, Iowa,-based radiation oncologist, author, and TEDx speaker I had the privilege of interviewing on my podcast.

"On a basic level, freedom to me means being able to live life on your own terms," said Koneru. "And I think that's very true when you look at it from a gross level, whether it's in business, whether it's financially speaking...having freedom on those levels allows you to live life on your own terms."

"But I think on a deeper level," he adds, "this is where I'm spending a lot of my work now, on the spiritual and psychological level...I think freedom on that level is as important, but we pay less attention to it."

What, exactly, does he mean by that?

"Living life in a sustainable way, where you can live it on your terms, but also be able to eliminate suffering and pain," he said. "You can have financial freedom and freedom on a gross level, but if you are a slave to your mind or your emotions and you're suffering, I don't really consider that freedom at that point."

How does Koneru blend this purpose, meaning, freedom,

and alleviation of suffering and pain? Some clues are offered on his Facebook page, where he recently quoted Jordan Peterson: "People will tell you that the purpose of life is to be happy, and those people are idiots."

Koneru went on to post, "The purpose of life is to be useful. You do this by carrying some responsibility for yourself and others. When you carry responsibilities it brings meaning. With meaning, you can weather the storms of life and may even get some fulfillment from that struggle."

He goes further in his 2014 TEDx talk "Empowering Those with Cancer."

"We as humans are very unique," said Koneru. "We have this propensity to survive, but at the same time, we have this really highly developed brain that understands we're going to die, even if it's not immediately."

As such, he said we create systems—society, culture, family, relationships—to provide us a level of "certainty" to get through life.

People who are truly fulfilled—those who change the world—he says, are those who follow the systems for a while but then break off to follow their own path and find their own purpose and sense of meaning.

How do they do it?

"First, you need a purpose. You need to know why you get up in the morning," he said. "And it needs to be one of a compelling future with hope."

"Second, you need morals and values...because we are wired for empathy," he added. "And third is significance. We need to feel that we're bringing some value into this world."

These three steps allow us to live that life of meaning rather than simply pursuing what Peterson says is the "instant gratification" of mere pleasure, which can lead to pain and suffering.

And the alleviation of pain and suffering is something Koneru contends is an important attribute of freedom.

So, yes, it takes more than freedom.

It takes the fulfillment of knowing your purpose and living a moral life, one of significance.

When you pair freedom with this fulfillment, you are truly living the Freedom Lifestyle.

CHAPTER 5

WHAT'S IT GOING TO TAKE?

What's your marriage worth to you? How about your relationship with your kids?

$1,000?

$5,000?

$50,000?

Most—I hope, all—of you think that's a preposterous question. The relationships with the people we truly love are priceless.

It's impossible to put a monetary value on them.

So you say...So you claim...

But then I meet people each week who do just that—without even realizing it. Here's what I mean.

One of the first questions I ask my potential clients is to paint a vivid picture of the lifestyle they want. Some have trouble doing this, while some can paint the picture with ease.

Many of them want a lifestyle in which they're more mentally and physically present with their spouse and with their kids. It's part of the lifestyle they want—but it's not part of the lifestyle they're living now.

Some of them tell me their current lifestyle, career, or workplace is impacting their marriage. It's jeopardizing their important relationships.

Many of these individuals are making $250,000-plus salaries.

And when asked what's holding them back from making a change, they often come back with a dollar amount.

"I need to make sure I keep my $XXX,000 salary."

So let's be brutally honest: that dollar amount is the price you've put on your marriage and relationship with your kids.

Hey, that's not fair! You might be saying to yourself, *But I'm doing it for my wife and kids...That salary is all for them!*

Well, let me ask you this: If you're making that salary now, and your relationships are suffering...

If you're making that salary now, and you're living in quiet desperation...

If you're making that salary now, and you're coming to me because you are clearly worried about losing the people or things you love...

Then that dollar amount you've named is absolutely the price tag you are putting on those relationships. Because if you truly value your relationship with your wife and your kids, you'll immediately put them ahead of money in the pecking order.

PAIN AVOIDANCE

Now, I don't write any of this to demean you. I'm not doing this to pass judgment. I'm writing it from experience. I'm writing it because I've absolutely been there.

I'm writing this because I'm heartbroken every time I see someone choose to remain in a comfort zone of misery—

jeopardizing their relationships—instead of standing up and fighting.

As I've mentioned previously in this book, a basic part of human nature is that we are often motivated more by pain avoidance than by the pursuit of happiness. Some people, more than others, let that pain avoidance mindset totally paralyze them.

If you're one of those people, clearly envisioning your perfect lifestyle isn't enough to get over the barrier of "perceived pain" you might have to endure to get to that lifestyle.

And, by perceived pain, I mean the what-ifs.

What if I work really hard to change, and I'm still stuck at the end of it?

What if I spend money on a coaching program, and it doesn't work?

What if part of my transformation involves quitting my job or having difficult discussions with people around me?

I could go on and on, but those what-if questions represent pain points that may happen. That's why it's "perceived" pain—but not enough to stop some people in their tracks.

So let's change the question.

Instead of asking you to define your desired lifestyle, I'm going to ask you:

What's your life going to look like if it continues down the current path?

What if it leads to further distance from your spouse?

Further distance from your kids?

What's your life going to look like if you add the loss of these relationships to your current anxieties?

The feeling of waking up each day and dreading your workday.

Weekends ruined because you're constantly worried about work, about money, about whatever?

Think about how much pain will be derived from that lifestyle.

Think of how much pain you're enduring now...and add to it.

How much pain will be derived from doing nothing?

The fact is, your short-term pain avoidance is setting you up for massive pain in the longer term. Are you waiting for massive pain to force your hand?

Recently, someone on LinkedIn tacitly admitted to me that he's waiting for the crisis to hit so that there's so much pain it forces him to invest in changing his life.

Quite honestly, that's what it took for me. The anxiety attacks, the snapping at my kids at the dinner table, the ruined weekends, the late nights...

None of it motivated me to change until it became so loud, so overpowering, that I shut down my profitable PR/ad agency overnight.

I've had some folks here comment to me that sometimes it's better to have a "lightning strike" moment like that to force change.

And yes, there was some benefit to being forced to swim without the benefit of a life preserver. But it doesn't have to be that way. If you really want to avoid pain, you'll begin taking action now to make changes in your life before it's too late.

If you really want to avoid pain, stop putting that salary-driven price tag on your most beloved relationships and make a change before you head off the cliff.

Know this: the earlier you act, the more likely it is that you can build the lifestyle you desire while strengthening your relationships and building the financial freedom that allows you to have the experiences that fulfill you.

IF YOU LEAVE YOUR TOXIC JOB, YOU'RE GOING TO DIE

Perhaps the lifestyle you desire means leaving your job. For years, you've felt trapped in a career, workplace, or job that leaves you unfulfilled.

But fear has held you back from making that change.

Fear of the unknown. Fear that you'll never have it as good in another job. Fear of money. Fear that you'll disappoint your spouse. Fear of the worst-case scenario.

What's the worst thing that could happen if you leave your job? You'll die.

And you know what? You will.

Actually, we all will. No matter what decisions we make

today, we're all going to die. Some of us may die later today. Some may die forty years from now.

But if you remain trapped in a life in which you have surrendered your fulfillment to your fears, you're dying a slow death inside that could leave you with decades of anxiety and regret.

It may sound macabre, but I often think about my death. It helps propel me forward. It helps me overcome my fear.

In fact, if you recall, it was that thought of death that finally helped me fire my biggest client and shut down my successful PR/ad agency.

That question I asked myself as I lay in bed on that Tuesday supposed-to-be holiday morning: If my plane goes down on the way to that God-awful meeting, is that how I want to go out?

The Hell, no! answer I told myself spurred me to change my lifestyle—a change that was long overdue.

Was making that change—shutting down my seven-figure agency at peak revenue—scary? Hell, yes.

But not as scary as the thought of my dying on the way to or from that meeting.

THIS FEAR IS MUCH BETTER

Looking back, the decision to shutter my agency was one of the best I've ever made.

There is still a fear that gives me drive—the knowledge that if I don't bring in clients, my family won't have income...and I won't be able to fulfill my vision of helping those individuals fight for lives of freedom and fulfillment.

But that is so much better than being driven by the fear of missing a call from a client, the fear of being scolded like a child at a meeting, or the fear that my family's financial survival hinges on the whims of clients who don't actually share my vision and values.

There will always be some type of fear in your life. The key is retaining power over your decisions instead of out- *or sponsors* sourcing them to employers or clients. You may think this sounds like a bunch of utopian bullshit. I get it. I once thought the same thing.

Until I got sick and tired of being a puppet whose strings were controlled by others.

Until I got sick and tired of being in a bad mood and mentally or physically not present with my family.

Until I got sick and tired of having to be on call during

my vacations or getting angry calls past 6:00 p.m. on a Friday about minor bullshit issues that could've waited until the next week.

That's when I decided to escape, and when I decided to help others do the same.

So when you say it can't be done, that's the fear talking.

If your current job has you trapped with golden handcuffs, that's actually fear that binds you.

The unknown always brings fear. That's why it's so vital to build an outcomes-focused life in which you live intentionally every single day to hit daily outcomes that move you toward your yearly objectives—and your life's vision.

More on living an outcomes-focused life later in this book...

ARE YOU THE REAL DEAL, OR FULL OF SHIT?

Sharing that motivational quote GIF on Facebook is going to change your life.

Making that LinkedIn video is going to finally give you purpose.

Trolling other people's content to tell them how weak and "dumb" they are is going to improve your life.

Now, of course, the above statements are total BS, but we all know that person (maybe it's you!) who exhibits that exact behavior.

They are the king or queen of the motivational memes—but in reality, we know their lives are a total mess. And they're either in denial about it, too afraid to make a change, or too stubborn to do so.

In other words, they're full of shit.

A BOT OR A HUMAN?

Technology makes it easier than ever to replace true action, engagement, and connection with things like "hashtag self-care" or "button-click advocacy."

Too many people limit their self-care to simply sharing motivational memes on Facebook...and then they wonder why their lives aren't changing for the better.

Why vote or help in your community when you can simply "like" the page of your favorite politician? (And I apply this to *all* political parties.) Why head to church when you can watch a thirty-second video of your favorite preacher on Facebook?

For many people, button-pushing has replaced engagement, connection, and community. It's also replaced good old-fashioned action.

Stop being a bot. Stop merely posting about change and wishing it would happen.

Make it happen.

A hashtag or a GIF won't save your life or the world around you, but getting your ass off the couch and living intentionally just might.

MEDIOCRITY LOVES COMPANY

In a recent LinkedIn article, Marcus Aurelius Anderson—whose incredible story of overcoming adversity inspires me every day—writes, "The gap between where you are now and where you want to be is separated by action."

"This action is inhibited by, you guessed it, fear," he continues. "Over time, this fear makes us compromise in every facet of life, and compromise leads to mediocrity."

Marcus writes, "Misery loves company, but not as much as mediocrity."

This, coming from a man who literally broke his back while preparing to deploy with the US Army and remained paralyzed for a year.

Marcus knows what fear is. He also knows the difference between someone who actually takes action—and someone who is simply full of shit.

Often, those pretenders talk a big game to fake a personal brand and hide the fact that they are scared shitless to get out there and actually play the game.

So they post. They comment. They publish.

And then they sit on the couch and do nothing.

They remain stuck in their comfort zone of misery.

IT'S TIME TO RECLAIM YOUR POWER

If you're in a career you hate, in a lifestyle that sucks, in a job that feels like a prison, admitting it—saying it out loud to someone else—is the first (and often the hardest) step. Remaining in your state of misery because of golden handcuffs, external expectations, or fear of change means you are willingly handing over control of your life.

It's time to reclaim that power. Then to find your purpose, your vision—the desired outcome you want for your life.

Imagine, whether you die later today or twenty years from now, that the person delivering your eulogy is allowed only one or two sentences to give it. What would you want those one or two sentences to be?

Do you want it to be that you lived a life of mediocrity? That you toughed it out in a shit job for twenty years? That you spent 3,750 hours a year commuting to a job you merely tolerated?

No. You don't want that. So what are you going to do about it? Are you going to continue pretending that you're fulfilled? Continue faking that you're living a life of power and purpose?

Or are you going to start being the real deal? Reclaiming your power today, defining your purpose, and setting big, audacious objectives that move you toward that purpose each and every year?

Whether you believe it or not, the choice is up to you.

DON'T BE CODDLED

In 2018, a potential client told me he didn't want to hire me because, as he texted me, "I like you, but you're a bit too angry sometimes and too critical of people who are just trying to figure shit out."

My response was, simply, "I'm not for everyone! Merry Christmas."

I meant it. My style isn't for everyone, and I'm fine with that.

One of my grandfathers lived with World War II shrapnel in his body until he died forty years after the war. My other grandpa was a World War I POW, during which he was forced to eat wild rats.

My father was diagnosed with cancer and given six months to live but kept swinging and lived for another two years.

My mom told me of growing up so poor she shoved newspaper in her shoes because her family couldn't afford new ones when the shoes got holes in them.

When I was in junior high, I was bullied because I was fat. Beat up. Called names. Instead of coddling me, my parents told me to eat better and exercise more.

That's how I was raised. So I'm glad the guy who sent me the text in the photo didn't join my coaching program. I coach out of love, and the greatest love I can show my clients is to not allow them to let BS excuses hold them back.

Today 6:14 PM

I like you but you're a bit too angry sometimes and too critical of people who are just trying to figure shit out. Best of luck in the new year!

I'm not for everyone! Thanks and Merry Christmas.

Delivered

I do not coddle.

Empathy is not the same as sympathy. I have much empathy for people, but I don't have sympathy for people who, of their own choosing, remain trapped.

"MISFIT" FREEDOM

Throughout this book, I've shared the stories of individuals who refused to remain trapped and overcame severe physical and mental roadblocks.

Marcus Aurelius Anderson. Caleb Campbell. Fraser Cameron. Tofe Evans.

Then there's Quentin Allums, whom I had the pleasure of interviewing on my podcast in January 2017.

"In my first year of entrepreneurship I took a dead-end job, saved money, quit that job, and jumped in full time," said Allums.

But his journey did not take an upward trajectory.

"My girlfriend left me, my dog was hit by a car [and survived], I totaled my car, and ran out of savings," he said. "I remember a point where I went to the grocery store, and I couldn't buy a $0.99 chocolate bar because I needed to buy my dog food. I was crying in my bed every single night."

He could've given up. He could've used the color of his skin or his age as an excuse. He could've shaken his fist at the sky and blamed God and folded up. But he didn't.

"I reached a point where I had -$900 in my bank account," he explained. "I spoke to my roommate, and I told him that if I didn't have at least one client by the end of the week, then I was going to quit and go get my job back."

What happened?

"At the end of that week I had three clients. I totally struggled after that. But that was the moment that I realized that someone like me could do this."

A few years later, Quentin is the CEO of the successful four-person, Milwaukee-based video production company Urban Misfit Adventures.

When I asked Quentin what the word "freedom" means to him, he replied, "It's being able to live my life in a way that I want to live my life, and that's every aspect: financial, my day-to-day, everything."

He added, "I want to be able to do whatever I want, travel whenever I want, but give back to people whenever I want. That's it. That's what I want."

Is he all in on the Freedom Lifestyle yet?

"I'm like halfway there right now," he said. "But we're getting there."

DRINK YOUR EGGS AND GO THE DISTANCE

In the fall of 2018, I had the pleasure of introducing my kids to the first *Rocky* movie. They had seen *Rocky III* and *IV*, and my daughter and I had recently watched *Creed II* in the theater.

But *Rocky* was the movie that started it all. And though it was the least "Hollywood" of all the movies, it was the best.

Here are three takeaway lessons I discussed with my kids after the movie, which I think are great for each of us to remember:

1. **Make the Decision:** When the promoter told Rocky they wanted him to fight Apollo Creed for the Heavyweight Championship of the World, he first says no. He's in disbelief. But it took him only a minute to reverse course, realize the opportunity he had, and say yes. He didn't overthink it. He took advantage of the opportunity and went for it.

2. **Drink Your Eggs:** He didn't take days or weeks to plan out his training schedule. He didn't delay for an endless stream of strategic-thinking sessions. He woke up early a day or two after making his decision, he cracked five eggs into a glass, and he drank them. That began his training to take on the heavyweight champion of the world. Then, of course, he hit the streets and the gym for a quick five-week spurt of training before his fight. Stop planning. Start *doing*.

3. **Go the Distance:** The night before the fight, Rocky tells Adrian that he's not sure if he can win, but he just wants to do what no fighter had ever done: go the distance with Apollo Creed. And that's exactly what

happens in the fight. It's a draw, but Rocky shocked the world by going all fifteen rounds with the heavy-weight champ.

Thirty years later, in the movie *Rocky Balboa*, he tells his grown son, "You, me, or nobody is gonna hit as hard as life. But it ain't about how hard you hit. It's about how hard you can get hit and keep moving forward, how much you can take and keep moving forward. That's how winning is done!"

Decisiveness, massive action, and the ability to take punches have been absolutely key in my entrepreneurship journey. I'm currently building my third profitable company, and over the years, I've been knocked down—but I'm still standing.

So if you've been putting off positive change in your life—fearful of stepping in the ring to create the lifestyle you desire, I have one question: Are you ready to get out of bed and drink your eggs?

If so, the rest of this book details a process to start throwing some punches.

Part II

WHAT ARE THE FREEDOM FIVE?

Through my personal freedom journey, the people I've worked with in my career over the past several decades, and the hundreds of people I've coached across the globe, I've concluded that there are five characteristics of people who live the Freedom Lifestyle.

Before I go there, however, I want to make something perfectly clear: this is an overall framework. The specifics of what's worked for me or anybody I've featured in this book may or may not work for you. The Freedom Five provide the blueprint, but a real transition to the Freedom Lifestyle takes some hard work, some soul-searching, perhaps some major shifts in your career and relationships, and the ability to make yourself vulnerable and try new things. That last part may sound cliché, but it's a common sticking point among people who want freedom but are stuck in a "but this is the way I've always done it" mentality.

One guy recently accused me (on social media, of course) of trying to push my values on my audience. His comments were in response to a video I made about the fact that I set a limit of twelve hours of work each week. In that video, I mentioned the importance of relationships in building a life of fulfillment and how I put my relationships with my wife, kids, family, and friends number one. For some reason, that was just too far a bridge to cross for this guy.

Citing Gandhi and Jesus Christ, he tried to make the case that some people simply don't need relationships to be fulfilled. Throughout this book, I've made the case of the importance of relationships, and I won't get into his ludicrous introduction of Ghandi and the Son of God into the debate—but he was convinced I was telling him that my lifestyle was the only path to freedom and fulfillment.

Nothing could be further from the truth. We each have our own unique talents. Our own unique purpose. Our own unique likes, loves, and hates. The Freedom Five take all of this into account and allow each of us to be the best of ourselves within a framework that provides some certainty and structure.

Remember the Freedom Index I discussed earlier in this book, and the ten questions that allowed you to determine that index? It's time to review your answers to those questions, look at your Freedom Index, and determine how the Freedom Five can help you move your Index to a perfect ten.

THE FREEDOM FIVE

The remainder of this book focuses on providing more detail and actionable steps on each of these five pillars of the Freedom Lifestyle:

1. Superpowers
2. Vision
3. Alignment
4. Outcomes
5. Flow

Now, let's dive in and discuss in more detail what each of the Freedom Five means and how you can use them to begin your transition to the Freedom Lifestyle.

CHAPTER 6

SUPERPOWERS

As I mentioned earlier, five years after founding my agency, I was overwhelmed and burned out despite the great revenue. I tried a number of self-help books and programs, but none of them worked. The problem with many of those books and programs is that they try to get you to mimic a system or process that works for somebody else. They try to get you to believe that just because a celebrity executive or CEO has a certain morning routine, that very same morning routine is guaranteed to make you more productive and give you freedom.

That's total BS. Each of us has our own unique styles, habits, and talents—there is no one size fits all.

Then I came upon Gallup's StrengthsFinder (now called CliftonStrengths) program. It really spoke to me because it's about finding the power that is already within you—

your strengths. I prefer to call them superpowers. And when you work in your "Superpowers Zone," you're more productive, your days flow instead of grind, you have a better quality of life, you're more efficient, and teams that are in their zone are more profitable.

In short, that StrengthsFinder program, which is part of my 30-Day Total Freedom Lifestyle Transformation Course, was the first step in getting me to a life of freedom.

UNLEASH YOUR SUPERPOWERS

The most dominant development model in our society, whether we're talking about parenting or schooling or even on the sports fields and courts, is something called the deficit-based development model. That model is simple: focus on your weaknesses.

This model starts getting drilled into us at a young age. Gallup's research finds that the great majority of US parents (77 percent) think it's more important to focus on the subjects in which their child/children perform worst instead of the ones in which they perform best.

We also see this in the workplace. So many people receive performance reviews in which there might be a paragraph or two of throw-away positive comments, but then several pages listing everything that employee did wrong. That is deficit-based.

It's like telling world champion and Olympic gold medalist Usain Bolt, "Your 100-meter time is great, but your mile time sucks. As such, we're not going to allow you to run the 100 meters anymore until your mile time gets better."

When I tell that to audiences, they laugh. But it's what we do with our kids, our teams, our employees, and ourselves every day. *Focus on fixing your weaknesses.*

Several decades ago, psychologist and businessman Donald O. Clifton started to ask the question, "What will happen when we think about what is right with people rather than fixating on what is wrong with them?"

Clifton was the father of strengths-based psychology. He ended up building the CliftonStrengths program for the Gallup organization. That assessment/program is now used by 90 percent of Fortune 500 companies as well as large and small businesses and individuals. They use the program to build strengths-based workplaces to get the maximum productivity and the maximum performance from their workers.

As management guru Peter Drucker once said, "Most

people think that they know what they're good at, but they're usually wrong, and yet a person can perform only from a position of strength."

When you complete the CliftonStrengths assessment, you'll reveal your talents. We all have talents—those naturally recurring patterns of thoughts, feelings, or behaviors that can be productively applied. I prefer to call talents your untapped superpowers.

They're not yet strengths or superpowers, as Gallup lays out a simple equation:

Talent × Investment = Strength

When you invest in your talents, use them every day, combine them with your knowledge and skills, and exercise them like you would work a muscle at the gym, they become stronger. They become your superpowers.

As Tom Rath, author of *StrengthsFinder 2.0,* says, "Having the opportunity to develop our strengths is more important to our success than our role, our title, or even our pay."

Now, a lot of people confuse talent with skills. They say, "Oh, I'm playing to my talents. I'm playing to my strengths," when really what they're doing is playing to their skills. Here's an activity to show you the difference:

- In your dominant hand, grab a pen or a pencil and write this sentence three times: "I use my strengths every day."
- Now, I want you to write those same three sentences with your nondominant hand.

What did you notice? When you write with your nondominant hand, it takes longer. It's not as much fun. It doesn't flow as much. It's slower. It's sloppier.

Your dominant hand, whether you are right-handed or left-handed, is your talent. Writing is a skill. See the difference? You can certainly be a good writer, whether you are right-handed or left-handed. That's the best way to look at your talents and strengths versus your skills.

A friend who was a former semipro baseball player once asked me to describe strengths versus skills.

"Were you a right-handed or left-handed batter?" I asked.

"Righty," he replied.

"What was it like to hit from the left side of the plate?" I asked again.

"I sucked. Couldn't hit," he explained.

"What would it feel like if your manager required you to hit from the left-hand side of the plate for the entire season?" I asked.

"I wouldn't hit. I probably wouldn't play," he said.

Exactly. Whether in school, at work, or at home, our managers often require us (and we often require ourselves) to do the equivalent of hitting from the left-handed side of the plate on a regular basis. Or, to use an earlier example, the equivalent of writing with our nondominant hand all day long.

Not fun, right?

So it's no surprise that Gallup has done studies over the last several decades and found out that people who focus on using their strengths every day are three times as likely to report an excellent quality of life. They're six times as likely to be engaged in their jobs. People who learn to use their strengths every day have 7.8 percent greater productivity.

People who work in this "strengths zone" are also able to get in the flow each day. We talk about flow later in this book, but it's that state of becoming so engrossed in an activity that you lose track of time. It's that feeling at the end of the workday that your day sailed along instead of having been a grind.

WHAT ARE YOUR TALENTS?

Gallup finds that every human has thirty-four talent themes (themes are basically the language of talent). For example, my top five talent themes are:

- **Learner:** I love the process of learning.
- **Context:** I look to the past for solutions to present/future challenges.
- **Activator:** I love to start and get going; I'm impatient.
- **Responsibility:** I have a strong sense of doing what I say I'm going to do and an expectation that others will do the same.
- **Intellection:** I need that quiet reflective time each day just to take it all in and process.

So every human has all thirty-four themes; they're just in a different order for each person. It's one thing that makes us unique. In fact, according to Gallup, the odds that you'll find another human with the same exact talent themes in the same order is *one in thirty-three million*. Even if you find that "talent twin," it's likely that they utilize their talents (if they use them at all) in much different ways than you due to their different lifetime of education, knowledge, skills, and experience.

It's also important to note that themes at the bottom of the list aren't your weaknesses; they're simply the talents you use less regularly.

Can you determine your talents even if you haven't taken the CliftonStrengths assessment? There are some activities Gallup provides to help us find some clues to our talents.

First, think back to a day when you were at your best. When the day felt like a "flow" instead of a grind. A day when you came home from work, sat down with a beverage in your favorite chair and thought, This day went well. What did you do that day that made you feel this way? As important, what did you not do that day that helped you feel this way? Think long and hard, and take an audit of that day. It's very likely that you spent that day in your "strengths zone," working on activities that allowed you to do what you do best.

I can't think of such a day

Second, take a look at the statements below and honestly think about whether each statement applies to you:

- ✓ I take a book on vacation.
- I learn best sitting in a classroom with other people.
- I get my best work done late at night.
- ✓ I love to tell stories.
- I prefer crowds to small groups.
- ✓ I feel refreshed after time alone with my thoughts.
- ✓ I can lose track of time when I'm organizing things.
- ✓ I work better under short deadlines.
- ✓ I make a to-do list on the weekends.

✓ • I like to start conversations with people I don't know.
✓ • I like to start projects.
✓ • I like to finish projects.
✓ • I like to present in front of a lot of people.
✓ • I prefer one-to-one meetings to large groups.
✓ • I'm impatient.
✓ • I seek out problems to solve.
✓ • I am driven by a desire to win.
✓ • I like to bring people together in agreement.
✓ • I'm very creative.
✓ • I like to consider all angles before moving forward.
✓ • I like discovering new things: new foods, new places to explore.
✓ • I'm known for having spontaneous chats with strangers.
✓ • I'm glad to be the subject-matter expert.
✓ • I like thinking about the past.
✓ • I prefer thinking about the future.

How much or little you agree with each of those statements is telling of what talents you possess. Are you a relationship builder? An executor? An influencer? A strategic thinker? Knowing and "naming" your talents is the first step toward unleashing your superpowers.

The next step is "claiming" your talent themes. When you take the assessment, you'll be provided with a number of reports—providing insights and action steps you can take to better understand and embrace your talent themes. You'll also have access to the *StrengthsFinder 2.0* e-book to help you further claim your talent themes.

The third and ongoing step is "aiming" your talent themes: pointing them in the right direction so you can use them intentionally every day—exercising them and turning them into full-blown strengths...or...superpowers.

CHAPTER 7

VISION

"Every single day that I get...it's something that I really, really cherish because I wasn't supposed to be right now, doing this particular interview with you," said entrepreneur Alain Kapatashungu, founder and CEO of the real estate app FrontDoor.

Talk about gratitude. Kapatashungu lives each day with the knowledge that it could be his last. Not because of a sense of fatalism, but because he grew up in a situation that he is fortunate to have even survived.

When he was five, he found himself living in Rwanda in the midst of what we now call the Rwandan Civil War. It was during that civil war that five hundred thousand to a million Rwandans were killed in a genocide of mostly Tutsi but maybe also Batwa Pygmy.

Born in the Congo, he moved to Rwanda when he was three or four years old because his mom was working as a diplomat in the Congolese Embassy in Rwanda.

"It's definitely a beautiful place," Kapatashungu told me. "My happiest memory, which is crazy, is actually tied to Rwanda because I can remember vividly how it was awesome."

Everything changed, however, on the night of April 6, 1994. It was during that evening that the plane carrying Rwandan president Juvénal Habyarimana and Burundian president Cyprien Ntaryamira, both Hutu, was shot down by a surface-to-air missile on its approach to Kigali, Rwanda. That assassination set into motion the genocide and the First Congo War.

"Once that happened, literally in a matter of hours, you could hear from in the street, people were gathering, people were starting to shoot all over the place, some of our neighbors unfortunately, they immediately got killed," he told me. "In a split second, I really appreciate and love my mum for that—like, she's an incredible woman—she just grabbed my sister and I, pulled us in her arms, and we literally start running. No clothes, no food, we just had a bottle of milk, and then we started running everywhere, and we actually were on the run for maybe two or three months."

They ended up at a UNICEF camp, where they remained for several weeks. His father was a professor of literature and living in France at the time, so it was only Alain, his mom, and his sister.

"It was really, really kind of an emotional journey because we didn't think that we were going to be able to make it through because there were no reasons why we should make it through," he explained. "Everybody around us was pretty much dying."

Despite the death and confusion around them, however, Alain and his family kept their hope.

"I can remember vividly, every single day my sister and I were just looking at all the planes taking off, and we were just kind of imagining, 'Oh my God, it must be great. Where are those guys going?'" he explained.

Escaping Africa on one of those planes was not only his goal, it was the desired outcome for his life. He could imagine it. He could envision it. It was what drove him forward every day.

Getting on one of those planes was his vision. Alain learned at that young age what many adults in our society have yet to learn: a life of freedom and fulfillment requires a clearly defined vision—the glue that holds together all of our daily, weekly, monthly, and yearly objectives for our lives.

It was that vision that kept Alain and his family moving forward, and it's a clearly defined vision that we all need to keep ourselves doing the same.

YOUR LIFE SENTENCE

Former Congresswoman Clare Boothe Luce, who later became an ambassador and author, was concerned that President John F. Kennedy was stretching himself too thin and setting himself up for disappointment and defeat.

She reportedly told him that the lives of all great men could be summed up in one sentence. She called that their "life sentence."

For example, can you tell me who she was talking about when she said the following:

He preserved the Union and freed the slaves.

Or how about this:

He lifted us out of a great depression and helped us win a world war.

Now, whether you agree with those statements or are a political fan of those people, you probably know who those sentences describe: Abraham Lincoln and Franklin Delano Roosevelt, respectively.

When you say those one or two sentences, most people know who you're talking about. That one sentence defines that person's life and legacy. That brings us to vision: the second pillar of the Freedom Lifestyle.

It is absolutely vital in living a life of freedom and fulfillment that you have a clear, compelling, and defined vision statement for your life. Whether you're going to die in twenty minutes from right now or twenty years, and the person at your funeral delivering your eulogy is only allotted one sentence, what is the one sentence you would want them to say that sums up your life or legacy? What is your life sentence? That's what a vision statement is.

I don't want a life sentence.

When I do workshops, invariably there is one person (usually a man) who shouts out that he would want to be said of him at his funeral that "He worked his ass off." Really? That's what you want the members of your surviving family, your wife, your kids, your grandkids to know about you?

Remember the story I told of my father's wake: when

after an incredible career saving the world, nobody really talked about his career. Instead, he was defined by his role as a husband, a father, a volunteer in the community. That's what freedom and fulfillment are all about. It's about a vision statement that doesn't just define you by your work or job title or paycheck, but defines you by your role as a family member, your relationships, and, yes, your work. That's why it's so important to have that clearly defined vision statement.

Now, when I say the words "vision statement," some of you may be thinking "mission statement." And perhaps that has a bad connotation in your mind, for good reason. I've had clients and been part of organizations that bring in very highly paid consultants to spend hours, and perhaps weeks, crafting an eight-page mission statement. In the end, it looks nice and sounds nice. Perhaps it's put in a nice frame and hung on the wall. Maybe it's put on a secondary or tertiary page on the company website. But after the consultant has cashed his or her check and is long gone, everyone forgets about that mission statement.

That is not what a vision statement is all about.

PURPOSE + IMPACT = VISION

We're going to talk more about outcomes later in this book, but your vision statement is the desired outcome you want for your life. A lot of people ask me if a vision statement is the same as purpose. I used to think it was the same, but after working with hundreds of people around the world and from my own experience, I have come to believe that vision is bigger than purpose. In fact, a compelling vision statement combines your purpose for living with the impact you want to make on the world.

Some people also are convinced that you should have multiple vision statements in your life. But they're confusing vision with objectives. Having yearly objectives, and maybe five- and ten-year objectives, is important. For example, when you're in your twenties, perhaps you think your vision is to make partner and earn $100,000 a year. Then when you get in your thirties, you think your vision is to find your mate, get married, and have kids. Those aren't visions; they're actually not even purposes. Those are objectives.

It's critical to have those objectives, but if you go through life from objective to objective without a clear and compelling vision that serves as the glue to hold them together so that you're moving in the right direction every day, every week, every month, every year—then at some point, you are going to find yourself lost. You are going to hit _No._ the wall—whether it's in your thirties, forties, fifties, or beyond—and have that feeling that you don't know what you were put on this earth to do.

Whenever you take a trip, you usually know the destination you want to go to, while also having milestones and landmarks in between. Whenever we drive back to Chicago, I plot out our rest stops, perhaps where we're going to stay overnight. Those rest stops and temporary stays are objectives, but I also have a clear idea of where I want to go. That's what it means to live an outcomes-focused life. We're going to talk about that later, but the important thing for you to realize is that a compelling vision statement provides your desired outcome for your life.

KEEP THEM THE SAIM

The other difference between a vision statement and a mission statement is that mission statements are long and bloated. Vision statements are short. I always say that you should keep your vision statements the SAIM:

- **Short:** Simple and simplistic. One or two sentences. It should be something that when people ask you what your vision is in life, you can rattle it off very quickly. It's easily remembered, not just by other people, but by you.
- **Aspirational:** Something to reach for, your purpose for living. You keep moving toward it so you can make that maximum impact on the world.
- **Inspirational:** When you tell people about it, they should say, "Yes, I want some of that."

- **Motivational:** Even on those toughest of days when you're lying in bed, you should be able to think of your vision statement; it should motivate you to blast through the day, to reach for your desired outcomes, to meet whatever challenges face you that day, week, or month.

VISION QUESTIONS

So you may be thinking, Well, coming up with my purpose and impact and a compelling vision is easier said than done. And you're absolutely right.

I once had a client tell me that coming up with a vision statement was easy, but coming up with one that he would "be happy to tattoo on his chest" was difficult. While I don't suggest that you tattoo your vision on your chest, your vision statement should be something that is permanent, something that you should be happy to share with the world, something that you should embrace and be proud of every day.

So here are some questions to help you craft your vision statement:

- What are your strengths, your superpowers that we talked about in the last section? How are you leveraging them? How do you wish you could leverage them?

- What are those one or two things you would want to be said about you at your funeral that would make you feel that you passed on a lasting, fulfilling legacy?
- What things, people, and activities make you feel the most passionate?
- Where would you like to be in five years? Ten years? Twenty-five years?
- If you found out you only had one week left to live, what are the one or two things you wish you would have done by now, but haven't?
- How does your vision align with your strengths? And on that last note, when you look at your strengths and superpowers, how can you use them to help craft your vision and achieve it?
- When you come up with your vision, is it one that is going to allow you to use those superpowers every day to achieve it?

Everything should be in alignment; each one of the Freedom Five pillars should work hand-in-hand and align with one another. They are cumulative; they should add up to help you live that Freedom Lifestyle you desire.

We'll meet Alain Kapatashungu again in the next chapter, but it's important to note that his vision, that desired outcome he imagined every day, was to get on the plane to freedom and life. Everything he did, every single day, led to that vision for his life. Now, decades later, it's clear that his vision is still freedom, life, and having the maximum impact he can on the world. The vision he adopted as a five-year-old has remained with him to his early thirties.

How did he adapt that—and how does he continue to do so—to ensure he moved/moves toward his vision every day? That brings us to the next pillar of the Freedom Five: alignment.

CHAPTER 8

ALIGNMENT

You're working long hours, and something's just not right. You have that sense of overwhelm, of frustration. You don't see your wife, your husband, your partner, or your kids enough. You don't have time to read that good book or even head to the gym.

You keep seeking "work-life balance." But the more you seek it, the more you attempt to achieve it, the further away it seems.

I'm sorry, but you're setting yourself up for a life of regret.

"Work-life balance" is bullshit. It's a myth. Here's why...

A WARPED VIEW OF BALANCE

When many people think of "work-life balance," they tell

themselves, I'll put my head down, not see my spouse or kids, work twelve hours a day, not sleep, and be miserable for a few weeks, but after that, I'll come up for air, take some time off, and it will all balance out.

Aside from the fact that there is no guarantee that you'll even be alive in a few weeks to enjoy that "balanced" time, that mentality often allows the "few weeks" to turn into a few months. Then maybe a few years. Before you know it, you're telling yourself that you'll come up for air in "another five or ten years." Perhaps when "I have enough money in the bank." Or perhaps "when I'm sixty-five and retire."

"I wish I could do what you did and just quit and gain my freedom," my former client told me shortly after I shut down my seven-figure agency. "You know I don't like this job, but I have young kids, and I just need to work a few more years to save enough money to move on."

I've heard at least a dozen versions of that story during the past year. I know—and that former client knows—that the "few more years" is going to stretch into a much greater period of time. Because if you constantly think you just need "enough money to move on," you'll likely never have enough money.

Remember, my wife and I put off our European trip

for seventeen years because we never had "enough money" to feel comfortable to take the trip—even when my agency was bringing in seven figures and I was having days in which I booked $300,000 in revenue!

There are so many people, just within my family or circle of acquaintances, who have fallen into this endless cycle of "balance chasing." The "few years" continues to expand until there is this false hope that age sixty-five will bring paradise and a period of endless bliss. But they get to be sixty-five and...they have to get a knee replacement (put the travel on hold!). Or they have a stroke. Or get cancer. Or have a heart attack. Or one of those things afflicts their spouse or children.

I don't write this to be macabre or alarmist. I write it because these are all things that have happened to multiple people I know!

There is no guarantee that you'll live to the end of today. There is no guarantee that you'll live to sixty-five. And if you're spending the prime health years of your life in a "wait to sixty-five" mode, you're not truly living at all. You're setting yourself up for the "Where did the time go?" freight train to hit you at some point in the future. You're building toward the desperate feeling that you missed seeing your kids growing up because you were too busy with your head down, building toward "balance" at some mythical point in the future.

You're guaranteeing that, at some point, you're going to wish you had traveled more, that you had worked out more, that you had spent more time with your kids, that you had invested in your relationships more.

Here's the deal: there's not work *and* life. There's just life, and how you choose to spend the time in your life is entirely up to you. The key to a life of freedom and fulfillment isn't balance; it's alignment—aligning the three facets of your life: family, self, and work.

YOUR REASONED CHOICES

The great stoic Epictetus wrote, "Who, then, is invincible? The one who cannot be upset by anything outside their reasoned choice."

One can take several meanings from that quote. For one thing, it strikes at those who allow their mindset and mood to be influenced by social media, by politicians' pronouncements, or by the goings-on of celebrities.

But I'd like to focus on his use of the term "reasoned choice." There certainly are things outside of our control. The weather. Disease. The place into which we were born. <u>Government shenanigans</u>. The list goes on and on. Do you spend time worrying about all of those things? Do you let those things impede your forward movement? Destroy your mindset?

Or do you focus on the things you can control? More importantly, do you actually realize all the things in your life that you do control?

When my father was told he only had six months to live due to bladder cancer, he could've chosen to shrivel up and spend the final six months of his life moping, angry, and not truly living. That would've been his choice. Instead, he chose to fight. He not only wanted to give it every shot to extend his time on earth, he wanted to do so while attending his granddaughter's wedding (which he did) and attending our kids' birthday parties (which he did), going to a few more Notre Dame football games (he did), and making sure my mom was set financially and physically (she needed a knee replacement, and he was there by her side for it).

There were days when he was miserable due to the cancer and the chemotherapy. But whenever you asked how he was doing, he always replied, "Fantastic!" That mindset and his mood were his choice.

He ended up living for two years—beating the doctors'

estimates—and doing so many fulfilling things over that time. He didn't have control over the fact that cancer attacked him. But he did have control over how he reacted to it. That was his choice.

Alain Kapatashungu didn't have control over the fact that he was five years old and living in the midst of the Rwandan Civil War. That wasn't his choice. It wasn't his choice that millions around him were being killed. But it was the choice of his mother, sister, and him to have a daily mindset that they "would not die today." It was their choice to keep moving forward, not simply stopping and resigning themselves to the fact that they would be killed in the genocide.

Things outside of our control impact each of us every day. We have no choice in those matters. But we do have a choice about how we will respond.

When I spoke about choice in a recent LinkedIn video and how I made a choice to shutter my agency, and my wife and I made a choice to move to a warmer climate near the beach, one commenter pointed out that not all of us have the ability to make those choices. Specifically, he noted he would love to leave New York City, but he "has" to remain there because of his elderly relatives and some other matters.

Are those important reasons to remain put and not move? Absolutely. But it is his choice to remain. They're not easy choices. They're not pleasant choices. But they are choices. Even the mere mindset shift in which you tell yourself, I'm here because I choose to be can be so empowering. It's liberating. It's a daily reminder that you are not simply a prisoner of circumstance, but you are a free human being of choice.

That same commenter asked me about alignment—asserting that "high-flying executives" are forced to work twelve- to fourteen-hour days and can't possibly experience life alignment each day. My response is simply this: nobody forces anyone to be a "high-flying executive." Nobody is forcing the law partner who rarely sees his wife and kids and is drunk too much and sick all the time to remain in his job. He may think he has no choice, but he's wrong. The life he leads and the job at which he works are his choice, 100 percent.

THE PIZZA PIE

So, realizing that you have a choice in the matter of how you lead your life and wanting to scrap the myth of "work-life balance" in favor of aligning the three facets of your life—family, self, and work—how can you tell which areas of your life might be out of alignment? The answer lies in a pizza pie.

That's right—the pizza pie has all the answers. Here's a quick activity to help you determine what areas of your life might be out of alignment:

- Grab a piece of paper and a pen. In the middle of the piece of paper, draw a big circle. That's your "pizza pie."
- The pie is going to have three slices: one for work, one for family, and one for self.
- But the size of each slice has to be in direct proportion to the actual time (including anxiety, stress, mindshare) you spend on each facet of your life.
- Go ahead and draw those slices.
- When you're done, look at those slices and reflect.
- Now, redraw the slices (right over your initial pie), but this time, the size of the slices should be in proportion to how you *want* your life to be.
- Now look at the difference between the size of the slices. Big difference? Now you know which areas of your life need to be brought into alignment.

There's no right or wrong answer in terms of how big each slice should be. What constitutes alignment for me doesn't necessarily mean alignment to you. Everybody is unique with unique strengths, family situations, and circumstances.

That being said, people with whom I do this activity usually feel that the "work slice" is too big—and the "self slice" is too small. When many people realize they need to invest more in that slice of self, they get a sense of guilt—guilt that they might have to steal time and effort from family or work.

A number of moms with whom I've worked really want to take some more time for themselves (at the gym, reading a book, going for a walk, or for coffee with friends), but they feel guilty about doing it. I've worked with some agency founders who cringe at the thought of taking more time for themselves for fear that taking their mind off their business for just a few hours a week will lead to the ruin of their enterprise.

Here's the deal: never, ever, *ever* feel guilty about investing in yourself, as long as it's in alignment with the other two facets of your life.

Investing in yourself means more rest. More relaxation. More time for learning—for thinking and processing your day. When you invest in your mental health and your physical health, your work and your family will be better off.

Your relationships will improve. You'll have more energy to focus on the things that are essential (and not just busywork) to scaling your business.

Stop chasing that mythical "work-life balance." Start
seeking alignment instead.

CHAPTER 9

OUTCOMES

We've revisited Alain Kapatashungu's story several times thus far. In the "Vision" chapter, we looked at how his clear vision to one day get on the plane to safety and freedom served as his desired outcome for his life. But he didn't just sit back and wait for that vision to come to him, letting hope serve as his only means of reaching it.

"I didn't know what I was doing when I was fleeing with my family, but basically we were literally persevering," explained Alain. "We had this idea of saying we are not going to die today, not this week, not this month. So what are we going to do about it? Well, we're going to persevere. We're going to walk some more. We're going to go without food this specific day, or we're going to sleep in places where you can't even close your eyes because you're afraid maybe those guys are going to find you there."

So many people are great at coming up with a big, audacious vision. They can picture it in their mind's eye. It makes them excited, perhaps uncomfortable, and maybe even a little embarrassed to tell their friends. But that vision never becomes a reality because they didn't have what Alain had every single day: a clearly defined outcome for every day.

Alain's was "We are not going to die today." And by achieving that outcome every day, it led up to his vision.

Outcomes is the fourth pillar of the Freedom Lifestyle because living a radically outcomes-focused life is so vital to clearly plotting your destination for your life, as well as every year, every month, every week, and every day between now and the end of that life.

THE TRUE DEFINITION OF PRODUCTIVITY

Let's start with the true definition of productivity, a word that doesn't mean what you likely think it does.

Too many people think the definition of productivity means "getting more stuff done." They wake up earlier, stay in the office later, cram more into their days, and then they call that "productivity."

In 2018, there was a hashtag campaign on LinkedIn called

the #5AMChallenge. The purpose of the challenge was to get more people to begin waking up at 5:00 a.m. As such, the social network was full of people posting pictures in front of their laptops or at coffee shops at 5:15 a.m. or 5:30 a.m. claiming they were boosting their productivity because they were working before the sun came up.

Sorry. That's not productivity. It's just getting more stuff done (and maybe not even important stuff).

Productivity actually means getting more of the *right outcomes* accomplished with *less effort*.

OUTPUT VS. INPUT

The actual definition of the word productivity is "the effectiveness of productive effort, especially in industry, as measured in terms of the rate of output per unit of input."

The rate of output per unit of input.

Notice the definition doesn't simply say "as measured in terms of units of input." It's all about the rate of output or, as I prefer to call it, *outcomes*.

Let's put it another way: true productivity is about finding the shortest, straightest, simplest route to your desired outcome.

Yet so many people think they're being productive simply by increasing the number of inputs in their day. Nope.

Knowing that, I must ask you: Were you productive today? Many times, when I ask that question, I get the following response: "Yes, I got a ton of stuff done today."

When I delve deeper, however, I find that "stuff" is simply defined as a long list of to-dos—many of which may not have an actual real impact on the outcomes that person is trying to achieve. Our days become defined by these task lists, where we are simply churning and grinding out inputs with no real progress toward a desired outcome.

The hamster keeps spinning, and the spinning seems to define whether we are "productive." It's complete lunacy. When many people are asked, "What's your secret to productivity?" they answer, "Well, I start working earlier" or "I get up at five a.m." or "I stay at the office later."

But are you getting the right outcomes done?

Have you defined clear outcomes for your year, your month, your week, and your day—and then reverse engineered them to determine the actual essential inputs that will most efficiently get you to those outcomes?

While we're talking about the meaning of words, let's also

talk about the popular term "grind." Entrepreneurs, business owners, and executives are told they have to "grind" to be successful. So many of them define their days and their "productivity" by how hard they grind.

When I worked in political campaigns, many "experts" would judge the effectiveness of campaigns by how late or early their campaign teams were working. That kind of mentality is what causes the caffeine- and Red Bull-fueled burnout culture in business startups. It's what leads so many people to fit five hours of work in a fifteen-hour day.

It's easy to become so focused on these external expectations or inputs that we lose sight of what defines real success: Are you meeting your desired outcomes? Because when you are working within your zone of strength, focusing on the essential outcomes, and auditing out all the BS inputs that waste your time and burn you out—you can get in the flow.

That's when you lose track of time because your work becomes almost effortless. You flow like water instead of grinding yourself into the ground (more on "flow" in the next chapter).

When you meet people who constantly say they are "too busy" (it may be you!), it's likely that they feel that way because their days are chock-full of BS inputs that may not make any sense given their desired outcomes.

When you change that mentality and begin making better choices about how you spend your time—you will feel like you are actually creating more time in your day.

THE PARETO PRINCIPLE

In the year 1897, Vilfredo Pareto, an Italian economist based at the University of Lausanne, published *Cours d'Économie Politique*, part of which made the case that 20 percent of the population of Italy owned 80 percent of the property. During the next century, this "Pareto Principle" was used to demonstrate everything from economic inequality to sales. According to Richard Koch's book *The 80/20 Principle*, "80 percent of sales come from 20 percent of clients."

In his best-selling book, *The 4-Hour Workweek*, author Tim Ferriss cites the Pareto Principle to make the case for true productivity.

"Pareto's Law can be summarized as follows: 80 percent of the outputs result from 20 percent of the inputs," writes Ferriss.

Obviously, I agree completely. When you set clear outcomes for your day and then reverse engineer them to plot the straightest, shortest, simplest line to those outcomes, you realize that about 80 percent of your day is total bullshit. The remaining 20 percent? Your outcomes-producing inputs.

Here's an activity you can try:

- For three straight workdays, keep a detailed time log. Be honest! *[handwritten: Then how can you lose track of time?]*
- At the end of the three days, list out all your activities (i.e., inputs) over that period.
- Then look at the actual outcomes you needed to achieve over that time period. *[handwritten: What if your work entails coming up w/ outcomes]*
- Which 20 percent of your inputs brought you 80 percent of the way to your outcomes?
- Now, look at the remaining 80 percent of inputs. How can you eliminate them, delegate them, outsource them?

[handwritten left margin: How do you concentrate on what you are missing?]

[handwritten: How do you measure the inputs when there's no unit of measure?]

I work with a number of entrepreneurs and C-level executives who, when I ask them to do this activity, tell me preemptively that I shouldn't expect to find any waste or "fat." I never believe them.

Most of the people with whom I work are entrepreneurs or C-level executives, and they either are trying to pack too many "to-dos" into their day, spending time on tasks that should be delegated, and/or spending way too much time on tasks in general.

They come to me for help because they know something's wrong. And despite their claims that their schedule is fat-free—we're always able to identify the waste that is causing them to spin their wheels.

MEASURE YOUR MILES

In 2018, I had a client who had set a New Year's resolution at the beginning of the year of traveling five hundred man-powered miles during the course of the year. This included hiking, walking, biking—any mile not powered by a motor or engine. We began working together in late July, and in late September, he told me of his resolution.

"How close are you?" I asked.

"Well, I just looked this week, and I'm only at 255 miles," he replied. "And the problem is that here in Montana, we get so much ice and snow in November and December that I expect those two months to make it tougher to travel those miles."

Obviously, he should've been at that halfway mark around July 1. But he hadn't been tracking his miles on a daily or weekly basis. He hadn't set daily, weekly, or monthly outcomes. Just the yearly. As such, he was far off his mark.

I challenged him to put together daily, weekly, and monthly mileage outcomes for the rest of the year. Long story short: he hit five hundred miles by the end of October.

Alain Kapatashungu would've never met his objective of escaping Africa if not for the daily outcome of survival.

We won't meet our yearly "mileage" goals—nor our life vision—without knowing our key daily/weekly/monthly outcomes.

DEFINE YOUR OUTCOMES

In my coaching course, we spend considerable time and effort working to clearly define my clients' vision statements—those one or two sentences they want to sum up their lives.

Yes, their "why"...their purpose.

And then, each year, we work to set very clear, specific objectives. Working backward, we then set very clear outcomes for months, weeks, and years so that every day, they are moving toward their yearly objective and their life's vision.

This all requires living each day with intention, setting clear outcomes for their day, and then defining the straightest line to those outcomes.

Too many people expect way too much from their day, planning the day (if even planning at all) for the best-case scenario instead of for reality. In short, they are hoping to accomplish way too many outcomes by cramming in calls, meetings, presentations, memo writing, commutes, etc.—the list goes on and on.

Even if we assume that you've cut out needless inputs, you should still aim to accomplish fewer outcomes in your day. Why? Simple—you're clogging the drain with too much crap.

You try to shove so many outcomes down the drain that everything simply stops flowing. When that happens, you're late for one meeting, and then a call, and then your lunch meeting—and next thing you know, you're getting home at 9:00 p.m., and you haven't really accomplished anything in your day.

Turn off the water. Step away. Grab your plunger.

You're expecting that you can accomplish way too much in the day. You're setting too many outcomes for the day. Remember the definition of productivity? It's not about cramming more stuff into your day—it's about doing less to achieve more.

When you define fewer outcomes for your day, you'll unclog the drain, and you'll find that you'll begin to achieve more every week. When you become intentional about your days and begin to define the outcomes that really, absolutely, positively matter—you'll find yourself doing less to achieve more.

And you'll do it in a way that feels a lot more like flowing than grinding. (A nice segue into the next chapter...)

CHAPTER 10

FLOW

A talent for "guiding water from one place to another" is one of the many skills Leonardo da Vinci claimed when applying for a job with Ludovico Sforza, the Duke of Milan.

Da Vinci made the claim despite the fact, as Walter Isaacson points out in his best-selling biography *Leonardo da Vinci*, "the artist/inventor...had done no hydraulic engineering." A fascination with water and how it moved, however, is a common theme throughout Isaacson's book (and da Vinci's life).

During the course of his amazing life, da Vinci had designed and proposed ways for cities to manage, divert, and utilize their waterways for everything from public health to transportation to fortification.

As Isaacson writes, the roots of da Vinci's fascination with the movement of water had much to do with what he saw as the stark similarities between the flow of the waters of the earth and within the human body.

"As man has a pool of blood in which the lungs rise and fall in breathing, so the body of the earth has its ocean tide which likewise rises and falls every six hours," writes da Vinci in a 1490s notebook entry. "As the blood veins originate in that pool and spread all over the human body, so likewise the ocean sea fills the body of the earth with springs of water."

In his now-famous notebook "Codex Leicester" (now owned by Microsoft founder Bill Gates), da Vinci writes, "The body of the earth, like the bodies of animals, is interwoven with ramifications of veins, which are all joined together and are formed for the nutrification and vivification of this earth and its creatures."

He continues that for the earth, "its blood is the veins of waters; the lake of the blood, which is throughout the heart, is the ocean; its breathing and the increase and decrease of the blood through the pulses in the earth is thus: is the ebb and flow of the sea."

Da Vinci also examines how certain obstacles would impact the flow of water below the surface, how they would change the currents, and the visual patterns created by the water.

In the flow of water, da Vinci saw one of the foundations of the health and life of the earth, the human body, and even of cities and towns. In fact, whether that water was impeded or allowed to flow naturally could determine the life, or death, of these entities.

FLOW SYSTEMS

More than five centuries later, author Max Borders further examines the impact of flow on the world in his book *Superwealth*. His purpose is to show the impact of flow on market economies and draws upon the work of Duke University physics professor Adrian Bejan, who writes that "living beings and inanimate phenomena" have what he defines as "flow systems" in common.

"Flow systems—from animal locomotion to the formation of river deltas—evolve in time to balance and minimize imperfections," writes Borders. "Flows evolve to reduce friction or other forms of resistance, so that they flow more easily with time. This view has been termed the constructal law, which Bejan first stated thirteen years ago."

In fact, Bejan, recipient of the 2018 Ben Franklin Medal

for constructal theory, writes, "for a finite-size system to persist in time (to live), it must evolve in such a way that it provides easier access to the imposed currents that flow through it."

The flow system can apply to anything in nature, including the human body. The idea is that systems work best when things are most easily allowed to flow from one point to another.

Borders applies the idea of "flow systems" to market economics. That is, the economy works best when it is allowed to flow like a river but stops up when too many obstructions (like a dam) are put in the way.

Can such "flow systems" be applied to our lives?

OPTIMAL EXPERIENCE

Long-distance running wasn't something that came naturally to me. I'm short, stocky, carry a good bit of muscle, and don't have the long, sinewy legs usually identified with long-distance runners. What I lacked in natural talent, however, I attempted to make up for in grit and mindset.

During our high school cross-country practices, I was always breathing a bit harder and my heart pumping a little bit more than my fellow teammates—even when I was tied with them or a bit ahead. The number of strides I took over a three-mile race was considerably more than most of my teammates.

In short, running long distances was more of a grind for me than more natural runners. There were those days, however, when everything came more easily. There were runs where I found myself in a total rhythm—when my strides, my breathing, my heart rate all seemed to be in sync. It was during those runs that I lost all track of time. Not only could I rip off fourteen, fifteen, or sixteen miles at a time, I did so in a seemingly effortless fashion.

It seemed as if there were no obstacles in my way. The wind, the ground, the weather, my lungs—nothing felt as if it was holding me back. In other words, I felt like I was in a state of...*flow*.

Hungarian-American psychologist Mihaly Csikszentmihalyi refers to this state of flow as one in which we have an "optimal experience."

"The key element of an optimal experience is that it is an end in itself," he writes in *Flow: The Psychology of Optimal Experience*. "Even if initially undertaken for other reasons, the activity that consumes us becomes intrinsically rewarding. Surgeons speak of their work: 'It is so enjoyable that I would do it even if I didn't have to.' Sailors say: 'I am spending a lot of money and time on this boat, but it is worth it—nothing quite compares with the feeling I get when I am out sailing.'"

In the case of my running, it was during these "flow runs" where I didn't dread being out in the cold, the endorphins were rushing to my brain, and I was just in a state of bliss. It wasn't about getting in shape, nor was it about winning a race. (In almost every case, my flow runs were alone.) It was about the very run itself.

Csikszentmihalyi wrote of these experiences as "autotelic."

"The term 'autotelic' derives from two Greek words, *auto* meaning self, and *telos* meaning goal," he writes. "It refers to a self-contained activity, one that is done not with the expectation of some future benefit, but simply because the doing itself is the reward."

He explains further, "When the experience is autotelic, the person is paying attention to the activity for its own sake; when it is not, the attention is focused on its consequences."

In a September 1996 interview with *Wired* magazine, he described "flow" as "Being completely involved in an activity for its own sake. The ego falls away. Time flies. Every action, movement, and thought follows inevitably from the previous one, like playing jazz. Your whole being is involved, and you're using your skills to the utmost."

How can we work to get ourselves in a state of flow? What are the characteristics of such an optimal experience? According to Csikszentmihalyi, there are eight such characteristics:

- Complete concentration on the task
- Clarity of goals and reward in mind and immediate feedback *Not necessarily*
- Transformation of time (speeding up/slowing down of time)
- The experience being intrinsically rewarding
- Effortlessness and ease
- Balance between challenge and skills
- Actions and awareness are merged, losing self-conscious rumination
- A feeling of control over the task

In order to live the Freedom Lifestyle, it's vital to be intentional about creating a state of flow as much as possible in our lives. Whereas it's become popular for pop psychology authors to talk about the importance of "grinding," it's actually much more important to spend your days "flowing."

The reason that flow is the final pillar of the Freedom Five is that it can result from the cumulative effects of adapting the other four pillars to your life.

- **Superpowers:** It's when you work in your "Superpowers Zone" that things come more easily to you. Remember, writing with your dominant hand is much easier, more efficient, and less sloppy than writing with your nondominant hand. This is a simple example of using your superpowers. You "flow" with your dominant hand, not so much with your nondominant one. You're able to do more challenging activities with greater ease, and it's when you're in this Superpowers Zone that you can lose track of time during the activity.

- **Vision:** A clearly defined vision provides great clarity in terms of your desired outcome for your life—and if it is big and audacious, as I've suggested, it is absolutely intrinsically rewarding.

- **Alignment:** The very notion of alignment implies a flow between the three facets of your life: family, self, and work. When you are fulfilled in your life, your days are certainly more intrinsically rewarding, and you have more of a sense of control of your days—rather than a feeling that any one facet of your life (namely work) is in control of you.

- **Outcomes:** The vision you've defined is the clear goal for your life. Building a radically outcomes-focused life ensures that you've got those rewarding goals set for every day, every week, every month, and every year. It's also about removing the needless inputs that dam up the rivers of your day. Remember: the key is finding the shortest, straightest, simplest line to your outcomes. In other words, making sure the river to your outcome flows freely.

Perhaps nobody summed this up better than Csikszentmihalyi himself when he wrote:

> Even the simplest physical act becomes enjoyable when it is transformed so as to produce flow. The essential steps in this process are: (a) to set an overall goal, and as many sub-goals as are realistically feasible; (b) to find ways of measuring progress in terms of the goals chosen; (c) to keep concentrating on what one is doing, and to keep making finer and finer distinctions in the challenges involved in the activity; (d) to develop the skills necessary to interact with the opportunities available; and (e) to keep raising the stakes if the activity becomes boring.

In other words, let your freedom flow.

IN CONCLUSION

THE FREEDOM MINDSET

"My father was a black pimp...a pimp and drug dealer."

—JT MCCORMICK

If I hadn't already read his book, JT McCormick's introduction of his childhood during an interview on my podcast would have stopped me in my tracks. Nonetheless, it was powerful to hear him tell his story.

"I was born in 1971, and my mother's white," he added. "Mixed race, in the seventies, not a good look, not accepted in this country, very looked down upon. And so, again, my father had twenty-three children. I'm one of twenty-three and needless to say, he didn't take care of any of us."

It was an inauspicious start to life for someone who has become a multimillion-dollar entrepreneur, CEO, speaker, and author.

"My mother and I were raised very poor, U.S. poor, let me make sure I say that," JT told me. "It wasn't an easy childhood. We lived on welfare. I make the joke, Curt, my mother and I never had these four things at the same time: money, food, water, or electricity. We were always missing one of those things. In most cases, we were missing two, but we were always missing one. We would always make the joke that we were so poor, we couldn't afford the 'o' and the 'r.' We were just 'po.'"

"But you know, it's...I look back, and I'm thankful for the things that I went through."

There it is again: gratitude. We've seen it again and again from the people whose lives I've highlighted in this book. And like them, JT didn't use gratitude as an excuse not to push for more.

"I was in juvenile three different times as a child. I was sexually molested from the ages of six, seven, and eight by one of my dad's prostitutes. I don't know where my last name comes from," he explained. "My mother was given the last name McCormick in the orphanage. She was raised in an old-school institutional orphanage. When she turned seventeen years old, they gave her twenty dollars, a small suitcase, and they said, 'Good luck' to her. Unfortunately, one of the first people my mother met was my very well-dressed, fast-talking pimp father, and here I am."

So JT clearly had a crappy childhood. Worse than many. Better than some. During the course of our interview, he even pointed out that he embraces the knowledge that, as bad as he had it, he knows there are people elsewhere in the world who had it far worse. Yes, that's gratitude.

"For me, I don't go with a victim mentality," he said. "As much as I sit here, Curt, and I ask, 'Okay, why was my father a pimp? Why did he have twenty-three children? Why was I sexually molested? Why don't I know where my last name comes from?' It doesn't change anything."

He continued, "I've never felt that I was a victim of anything. If you get caught in a drive-by, yeah, you were a victim of a drive-by. You didn't expect that. If you were caught in a hit-and-run accident, you were a victim of a hit-and-run accident. I had a challenging childhood. That's all it was. Were some of the things very disturbing and graphic? Oh, yeah, for sure. But here's what I realize: I can't change it. I cannot change anything from my past. So I choose to focus on what I can change, so I don't sit back and ask a lot of whys.

But his gratitude is mixed with a good dose of abundance mindset, which has been powerful in moving him beyond his challenging upbringing.

"I even remember my mother, as a child on days where we didn't have anything to eat or maybe the electricity was cut off. My mother would always tell me, 'You know, there's people worse off than us,'" he said.

"And even then, Curt, my mind as a child was, 'Yeah, but there's people better off than us, as well, and I wanna focus on them.'"

Throughout this book, I've shared the stories of individuals who faced a variety of struggles. Some, like JT's or Alain Kapatashungu's, seem unbelievable to most of us. Others, such as mine or Fraser Cameron's or Tofe Evans's, might seem more relatable. Marcus Aurelius Anderson's seems downright heroic.

As JT discussed with me, everyone has a story. And one person's challenges are no better or worse than someone else's. Our stories make us who we are.

In every case, though, there was a catalyst for change. For me, it was my father's death and the anxiety attacks. For Fraser, it was his son asking him why he was grumpy all the time. For Tofe, it was the thoughts of suicide. For Marcus, it was being paralyzed for a year.

For JT and Alain, their catalysts happened at a young age. They were born and raised into their circumstances and forced to sink or swim despite their circumstances.

Everyone discussed in this book utilized an abundance mindset to empower change. They have all (without realizing it) used the pillars of the Freedom Five—superpowers, vision, alignment, outcomes, and flow—to build freedom in their lives.

But they all needed something else. We all need something else to finally make that decision to consistently build freedom in our lives.

I call it the Freedom Mindset.

"Life is not Instagram," said JT. "And what I mean by that, we now live in this society where people see the big house, the big car, the money, and they feel as if it's that easy. It's not that easy. You will go through hard times, but it's what you do with it during those hard times and the mindset that you take."

He explained further, "Every day at four a.m., the alarm clock goes off. There are days, Curt, I'm human, I don't wanna get up at four a.m. I wanna stay in bed. I wanna go back to sleep."

"On those days, I take the mindset and I say to myself, Okay, somewhere right now, in Austin, someone is in a hospital bed with cancer that's never gonna leave that hospital bed," he said. "They would give anything to get on their own two feet and just walk to the restroom and have the dignity to use the restroom on their own versus in the bed. All I gotta do is get up in the morning and go achieve my dreams and goals? I've got four beautiful children, a lovely wife, a beautiful home. I jump out of bed; that's the mindset I adopt."

For JT and the others I've described in this book, the Freedom Mindset is about more than just positivity. It's about making the choice that you're in control of your life and your destiny. It's about deciding that you're going to happen to life, rather than let life happen to you.

"I did not create the rules of society," said JT. "But I'll be damned if I was gonna let society hold me back. And I was gonna find a way to understand, learn, figure out how can I navigate society to make it work for me and do so in a positive manner."

And make it work for him...he did. He decided to do so at a young age.

"When I was ten years old, I lived in Houston, Texas, with my father. And I don't know that he ever realized he did this for me. Maybe he knew what he was doing," he explained. "He drove me through a community called River Oaks, and it's a very exclusive neighborhood community in Houston, Texas, and it was the first time I had seen ten-, fifteen-, twenty-five-million-dollar homes. They were bigger than the projects that I grew up in, and I remember saying to myself, I want one of those houses."

And you know what? He made it happen.

Whether you are born into a challenging world, or whether you create a challenging world for yourself through the choices you make—it's always possible to make the decision to fight for freedom.

I'm not saying it's easy.

It may not be pleasant.

It might even take some days when your desired outcome is simply to survive.

But in every case, it takes a conscious choice to adopt a Freedom Mindset.

It requires a mindset of abundance instead of scarcity.

From there, you can follow the roadmap I've laid out in this book, known as the Freedom Five:

- Unleashing your superpowers, and amplifying them every day
- Defining a clear vision for your life
- Aligning the three facets of your life: family, self, work
- Adopting a radically outcomes-focused life
- Getting into a state of flow as many days as possible

Thank you for allowing me to be a part of this journey with you. If you truly desire a life of freedom and fulfillment, I must ask...

What are you waiting for?

ACKNOWLEDGMENTS

I've wanted to write a book since I was about six years old. Thirty-eight years later, here it is. It's a lot more challenging than I thought it'd be, and so I want to thank everyone who contributed to the completion of a book I know will help empower and inspire people to live lives of freedom and fulfillment.

First, I want to thank my wife, Julie. She has been my rock since we first met. In this book, I write about the day I decided to transform our lives by shutting down my profitable agency. Her response, "It's about time," says it all. She is my teammate, my daily coach, my voice of reason, and my best friend. I love her with all my heart and am so very fortunate to share life's adventures with her.

I also want to thank my four children: Anna, Dominic, Rocco, and Santino. As their parent, and especially since we homeschool, I am one of their teachers. But they are also mine. I learn from them every day what it means to live with a sense of wonder, discovery, and excitement. They teach me patience, love, and what freedom truly means.

I'm eternally grateful to my mom. When I was probably six years old, I was bullied because I was, well, a fat kid. When another kid, Wayne, hurled some insults my way on the school bus, I smashed him in the mouth with my metal lunchbox. My mom wasn't upset with me, though she made me apologize. My mom always taught me to stick up for myself and to not take shit from anyone. She's had a challenging life, and I've never once taken for granted how hard she worked to make my life better. Thank you, Mom. I love you with all my heart.

I write about my dad in this book, who was my superhero. My mom has a little note in her house that says WWND (What Would Nick Do). I have a constant voice in my head that says WWDD (What Would Dad Do). My dad was larger than life and was the family leader. Someone recently asked me the best piece of advice anyone ever gave me. My reply was my dad telling me, "Now go out there and kick some ass." I'm trying, Dad. I'm trying.

I'd also like to thank my coach and close friend, Fraser Cameron. I wrote about Fraser in this book. He helped me through my freedom transformation and pushed me to get this damn book finished! As you read in this book, his story is an inspiration.

Thank you also to Susan Rooks, who made me look good by editing the hell out of my first three drafts of this book! Susan and I clicked because we both have a "no bullshit" rule. Thank you, Susan! I hope we did you proud!

Thanks also to JT McCormick, who is not only referenced in the conclusion of this book but who taught me about Scribe Media, my publishing company. JT's story floors me (in a good way) and inspires the hell out of me every time I read it. Thank you, JT, for being you—and for telling your story to help others. Thanks, also, for introducing me to Scribe!

ABOUT THE AUTHOR

CURT MERCADANTE is a speaker, coach, and social influencer whose mission is to save the world by helping individuals fight for lives of freedom and fulfillment. Curt hosts the *Freedom Club Podcast* and created a network of events around the country called "Freedom Club Local." Curt was raised in the Chicago area and is a graduate of the University of Iowa. He and his wife, Julie, reside in Charleston, South Carolina, with their four children. Last but not least, Curt is a diehard fan of the first Chicago-based MLB team to win a World Series this century—the Chicago White Sox.